TRANSCENDENCE-PERFECTION

THE WORKS OF SRI CHINMOY

TRANSCENDENCE-PERFECTION

★

LYON · OXFORD
GANAPATI PRESS
XCI

© 2022 SRI CHINMOY CENTRE

ISBN 978-1-911319-39-9

FIRST EDITION WENT TO PRESS ON 1 JANUARY 2022

TRANSCENDENCE-PERFECTION

1. ETERNITY'S VISION-REALITY SONG

Beloved Lord Supreme,
Do You approve of
My self-transcendence song?

"My son, not only do I approve
But it is I who will
Sing in you,
Sing through you
My Eternity's Vision-Reality Song."

2. HE IS REALLY SOMETHING!

He is really something!
He always likes to compete
With himself and
Transcend himself.

God smiles with joy
Because he competes
With himself.
God cries with joy
Because he does really
Transcend himself.

3. STOP AND START

Stop talking,
Start meditating!
Stop meditating,
Start serving!
Stop serving,
Start self-giving!
Lo, your cosmic game is over!

4. TWO SIMPLE PROMISES

Two simple promises
To God
To remember:
God, I shall love You
Unconditionally.
God, I shall please You
Eternally
In Your own supreme way.

5. SURRENDER-TEARS

If my life's freedom dies,
What shall remain
In my heart?
Not the sighs of loss,
But the illumining
Surrender-tears
Of my gratitude-soul.

6. YOUR GOD, HIS GOD, MY GOD

Your God tells you
To love Him.

His God tells him
To serve Him.

My God tells me
Not only to claim Him
But also to equal Him.

7. WHO WANTS?

Easy life of the cosmic gods
Who wants?
Me? Never!

Peace-Light boundless of the cosmic gods
Who wants?
I want,
I wanted,
I shall always want!

8. HAPPY AND UNHAPPY

Happy you are
With your life's sincerity-cry.
Unhappy you are
With your heart's insecurity-sigh.

9. HE ASKED GOD WHO HE WAS

In the small hours
Of his earthly life
He asked God
Who he was.

God answered in the evening
Of his life:
"God's transcendental Silence-Vision
And
God's universal Sound-Reality."

10. TO DESCRIBE HAPPINESS

To describe happiness
Is to make friends
With impossibility.

To describe happiness
Is to exhibit one's
Stupidity's reality-existence.

11. IMAGINATION AND REALISATION

Imagination
I had.
God took it away
And
Gave it away.

Realisation
I have.
God adds His own Realisation
To mine and says:
"Son, promise that you will
Always
Stay with Me,
In Me
And
For Me."

Father, Amen, a thousand times.

12. THREE POPULAR ERRORS

Three very popular errors:
God does not need me,
God cares only for others,
God is other than my own Reality-Existence.

13. THE SAINT AND THE RASCAL

When the saint looks
At temptation-beauty
He becomes a real rascal.

When the rascal enjoys
Illumination-liberty
He becomes a real saint.

14. HE AND SLEEP

He has surrendered to sleep;
Therefore
His name is incapacity-ant.

Sleep has surrendered to him;
Therefore
God requests him to accept
God's infinite responsibilities.

15. I LOVE ONLY ONE THING

I love only one thing:
I love to be superior
To my yesterday's realisation
And
To my tomorrow's expectation.

16. IDLENESS AND INCAPACITY

Idleness feeds incapacity
To increase its incapacity-hunger.
Incapacity gladly surrenders
To the whims of idleness-prince.

17. I CAN ONLY PROMISE

I can promise
To be sincere;
But sweet Lord,
It is You alone
Who have to make me sincere.

I can promise
To be good;
But beloved Lord,
It is You alone
Who can and will
Make me eternally and supremely good.

18. THAT IS NOT YOUR TASK

Don't overestimate
Your capacities.
That is not your task.
That is the task
Of God's fondness for you.

Don't underestimate
Your capacities.
That is not your task.
Your foes will do it for you.
In fact, they have already done it.
I must add, successfully, too.

19. EARTH-GLORIES AND HEAVEN-GLORIES

His confidence in himself
Aims at earth-glory.

His surrender to God's Will
At once
Transcends all earth-glories
And
Captures all Heaven-glories.

20. ADVICE OF A GOD-REALISED SOUL

Only one word of advice from a truly
    God-realised soul:
"O disciples of mine,
In stupidity
I have surpassed all donkeys
In God's creation put together
By becoming
A Guru.
I pray to you
Do not play this role of stupidity-sea."

21. TWO THINGS I SHALL HAVE TO REALISE

To see the inside
Of everything,
Two things I shall
Have to realise:
Everything is of my silence-height
And
Everything is for my realisation-light.

22. CITIZENS OF MY WORLD

Promise was a citizen
Of my previous world.

Hope is a citizen
Of my present world.

God-Compassion and self-confidence
Will be the citizens of my future world.

23. FINITE ACCOMPLISHMENTS

When he stands
On the stage of finite accomplishments
He feels happy,
Not because he has
At least done something,
But because this is what
His God wants him to accomplish.

24. WHEN IDEAS TRAVEL

When
Ideas travel forward
They really look beautiful.

When
Ideals travel upward
They really are fruitful.

25. TO OWN A LIVING GOD

To own peace
Is to own a living God.

To own a living God
Is to become another God.

26. AN EXCHANGE

All my mortal moments
I have finally surrendered to God,
Although hesitantly.

In return
God has granted me
His Eternity's Time-Satisfaction,
Cheerfully and unconditionally.

27. THE SWIMMER

He swims
In the ocean of hope.
He swims
In the ocean of failure.
He swims
In the ocean of tears.
Something more:
He swims also
In the ocean of his surrendered will
To his earth-Heaven-life's Pilot Supreme.

28. THREE METHODS

The human method
Begins by doubting.

The divine method
Begins by loving.

The supreme method
Begins by serving,
Unifying
And
Becoming.

29. A MAGNIFICENT LIE

Earth has told
A magnificent lie:
God is only for Heaven's beauty-smile.

Heaven has told
A magnificent lie:
God is only for earth's self-imposed
  insecurity-cry.

30. HE ROAMS

From hope to hope
He helplessly roams.

From frustration to frustration
He hopelessly roams.

From destruction to destruction
He unconditionally roams.

31. HIS HEAVEN-LIBERTY

Alas,
His Heaven-liberty
Has compelled him
To become inseparably one
With earth-responsibility.
Alas, alas!

32. WHEN BELIEF IS IN PROGRESS

When
Belief is in progress,
Life-boat sails
Very fast
And
God says:
"O seeker, just wait!
You do not have
To take any more trouble.
I am bringing the shore to you."

33. GOD'S ABSOLUTE SATISFACTION

Life-rejection
Is human fear.

Life-acceptance
Is divine strength.

Life-perfection
Is God's absolute Satisfaction.

34. THREE MEN I NEED

The man of imagination
I need
To fly in the sky.

The man of realisation
I need
To see the Face of God.

The man of perfection
I need
To satisfy God.

35. LEARN TO CONQUER

Learn to conquer.
Conquer what?
Conquer the animal in you.

Learn to fight.
Against what?
Against the human in you.

Learn to surrender.
To what?
To the divine in you.

36. ONE QUESTION REMAINS

One question
Remained,
Remains
And will always remain
Unanswered:
Who is *not* God?

37. BEAUTY, LUSTRE, ONENESS

Beauty
Is earth-satisfaction.

Lustre
Is Heaven-perfection.

Oneness
Is man-liberation.

38. FOUR PETALS OF DELIGHT

Four petals of delight:
Love-beauty,
Surrender-duty,
Perfection-necessity,
Oneness-immortality.

39. GREATNESS AND GOODNESS

You live in golden tomorrow;
You are divinely great.
He lived in golden yesterday;
He was divinely great.
I live in golden today;
But I am not divinely great.
Why?
Because my Pilot Supreme tells me:
Greatness is not satisfaction;
Goodness is not only satisfaction
But perfection itself.

40. A SAD WORLD-CRY

A sad world-cry
I hear and near.
A dead world-hope
I carry untiringly
To the destination-shores
Of Nowhere.

41. THE DEFINITION OF LOVE

Kill and be happy.
Indeed,
This is the definition
Of animal love.

Possess and be happy,
Indeed,
This is the definition
Of human love.

Become one and be happy.
Indeed,
This is the definition
Of divine love.

42. MY DAYS OF SWEETNESS

My days of sweetness
I have totally lost.

My days of sadness
I have somehow rediscovered.

My days of goodness
Will be found
Perhaps
Only in God's Compassion-Haven.

43. NOTHING IS PERMANENT

Nothing is permanent on earth.
No, not even your wild
Ignorance-night
And the long-forgotten story
Of your own
God-Oneness-Perfection.

44. HER BODY AND HER SOUL

Her body
Is the perfume of God-Sacrifice.

Her soul
Is the perfume of God-Ascendance.

45. ONE LITTLE DROP

One little drop of light
From her smile
Saved earth,
Immortalised Heaven,
Fulfilled God.

46. DO YOU WANT?

Do you want
To entertain my eyes?
Then dance.

Do you want
To feed my soul?
Then meditate.

Do you want
To love the real in me?
Then become a conscious
And constant friend
Of my Inner Pilot.

47. HER LIFE'S PERFECTION

Her life's perfection
Lets God in.
Earth needs
Her perfection-height.
Heaven needs
Her compassion-might.

48. HIS ALL-CONQUERING WILL

His thoughts began to cry
When they saw the face
Of his all-conquering will.
Lo and behold!
His all-conquering will
Has surrendered unconditionally
To God-satisfaction
For his own perfection-delight.

49. STAY WITH ME

My sweet Lord,
Don't withdraw
If You want me to live.
Stay with me.
Satisfaction grows
On patience-tree.

50. MY DAILY MEDITATIONS

In my morning meditation
I see God's Beauty.

In my afternoon meditation
I become God's Duty.

In my evening meditation
I surrender to God
For His transcendental Satisfaction,
My experience-reality.

51. OUR TASKS

My task is to meditate.
Earth's task is to wait and see.
Heaven's task is to smile.
God's task is to cry for me
And
Smile through me.

52. OUR MOUTHS ARE SHUT

Heaven's mouth is shut.
It will not criticise
Earth any more.

Earth's mouth is shut.
It will not insult
Heaven any more.

My mouth is shut.
I will not judge
Either Heaven or earth any more.

53. I CAN ETERNALLY BECOME YOURS

My sweet Lord,
Your Footprints
On the tablet of my heart
Make me feel that
I can not only become great and good,
But I can eternally become Yours,
Only Yours.

54. THE ANCIENT MAN

The ancient man
Needed God's Grace.

The modern man
Needs God's Face.

The future man
Will need God's Embrace.

55. A SACRED GIFT

A sacred gift of earth-tears
God treasures
Infinitely more
Than he treasures
A secret gift of Heaven-smiles.

56. COMPENSATION

Just because
To himself he is unjust,
God gives him
God's Eternity's Love,
God's Infinity's Delight,
God's Immortality's Life.

57. HUMAN WINNER, DIVINE LOSER

The human winner's cry:
"Not satisfied!
I need more!"

The divine loser's smile:
"My Lord Supreme has given me
What the soul in me
Really needed."

58. RETROGRESSION

Yesterday
You had the strong desire
To please God.

Today
You have the strong desire
To see God.

Tomorrow
You will have the strong desire
To become another God
Without pleasing, without seeing God,
Alas, alas!

59. THEY ARE BOTH EQUALLY RIGHT

My aspiration says:
I need God.
My Realisation says:
God needs me.
They are both equally right.

60. MY COURAGE

My body-courage
Dares to die.

My soul-courage
Dares to live.

My realisation-courage
Dares to surrender
Cheerfully,
Unconditionally,
To God's Satisfaction-Will.

61. BECAUSE HE DOES NOT COMPETE

Because he does not compete
Earth laughs at him,
Heaven feels sorry for him,
God in supreme secrecy prepares him
To compete
In the near future.

62. YOU FAIL AND GOD FAILS

You fail to honour earth's humanity;
Therefore
God fails to treasure your divinity.

You fail to honour Heaven's divinity;
Therefore
God fails to protect your humanity.

63. GOD'S RETIREMENT SPEECH

When a man's higher nature
Comes forward,
God tells him:

"Son, I am tired.
I have worked very hard.
I am retiring.
To you I give My Justice-Throne
And My Compassion-Crown
To guide and lead humanity
To My Golden Shore."

64. NO, NEVER!

Can sincerity-heart go to waste?
No, never!

Can humility-life be undervalued?
No, never!

Can purity-aspiration remain unrealised?
No, never!

65. SURRENDER-HEART ALWAYS WINS

Cleverness-mind never wins,
Skill-life at times wins,
Surrender-heart always wins
God's Pride
Of the ever-transcending Beyond.

66. THEREFORE GOD LOVES YOU

Your face is your heart:
Therefore
God loves you so dearly.

Your heart is God's Voice;
Therefore
God loves you unreservedly and
  unconditionally.

67. THE MAN OF GOD

The man of God
Is the vision-seed
Of God's Compassion-Height
And
The reality-fruit
Of God's Satisfaction-Delight.

68. SOMEDAY

Someday I will cry for You.
Today will You not cry for me, Lord?

Someday I shall really love You.
Today will You not love me, Lord,
Even for a fleeting second?

69. OPEN MY DOOR, PLEASE

Open my love-door, please Father.
I want to see You.

Open my devotion-door, please Father.
I want to manifest You.

Open my surrender-door, please Father.
I want to satisfy You.

70. NO COMPROMISE

No compromise, no compromise,
Either with earth's selfishness-night
Or
With Heaven's indifference-sky.
No compromise, no compromise!

71. ALAS, I AM SLEEPING

Alas, I was sleeping.
In vain God came and sat beside my bed.

Alas, I am sleeping.
In vain God comes to see me.

Alas, I shall be sleeping.
In vain God will be thinking of me.

72. YET GOD LOVES ME

I have no boat.
Everybody else has one.
Yet God loves me.

I have no boatman.
Everybody else has one.
Yet God loves me.

I have no goal.
Everybody else has one.
Yet God loves me.

Why does God love me?
Because His is the Life
Of unconditional Compassion.

73. COMPLEMENTARY BROTHERS AND SISTERS

World's two great
Complementary brothers:
Doubt and anger.

World's two great
Complementary sisters:
Stupidity and insecurity.

74. LORD, CALM THEM

Lord, calm my mind-horse,
Calm my vital-bull,
Calm my body-elephant.
I tell You,
If You can make them calm,
They can and will
Do much for You.

75. REPUTATION

Reputation is a great hindrance.
My disproportionate success-life
Knows it.

Reputation is not at all a hindrance.
My timely, proportionate progress-life
Knows it and will always remember it.

76. DON'T DELAY!

Taste nectar-light.
Don't delay!

Choose God-Embrace.
Don't delay

Become God-Perfection.
Don't delay!

77. WHO MEANS MOST TO YOU?

Who means most to you?
If God,
Then give Him
What you are:
His Silence-Smile.

Who means most to you?
If man,
Then give him
What you have:
Constant hope, constant frustration.

78. YOU ARE NO LONGER UNPARALLELED

Heaven,
Just like you
Earth was the other day
Smiling triumphantly.
Therefore
You are no longer unparalleled.

Earth,
Just like you
Heaven was the other day
Crying helplessly.
Therefore
You are no longer unparalleled.

79. ON ONE CONDITION

Lord, do stay with me.
"On one condition, son:
You will play with Me,
Always play with Me, son."
On one condition, Father:
You will employ me,
Always employ me.

80. THE EASIEST PATH

The easiest path:
The path of surrender-light.

The easier path:
The path of dedication-right.

The easy path:
The path of concentration-might.

81. INSECURITY LOOMS LARGE

Insecurity looms large
When impurity divides
Body and mind
From Perfection's oneness-reality.

82. HOW CAN I BE WITH YOU ALWAYS?

How can I be with you always?
Just by thinking?
Then I shall always
Think of you.
Just by loving?
Then I shall always
Love you.
Just by pleasing?
Then I shall always
Please you.

83. YOUR HUMILITY

You are really great.
Your humility
Has erased earth-anger.

You are really good.
Your humility
Has fed Heaven-hunger.

84. HOW I NEED YOU!

How I need Your constant love,
Sweet Lord!
Your Love is my heart's only food.

"How I need your constant service,
Dear son!
Your service is My expansion-perfection."

85. MY FIRST AND LAST COMMITMENT

My first and last commitment to man:
I shall love him,
I shall always love him.

My first and last commitment to God:
I shall always love, serve
And fulfil Him
In His own Way.

86. THE SURRENDER OF CONFIDENCE-LIGHT

Worse than depression
Is doubt-poison.

Better than joy
Is the surrender
Of confidence-light
To the Will
Of the Pilot Supreme.

87. LIFE'S SURRENDER

Better than heart's joy
Is life's surrender.

Better than life's surrender
There was nothing,
There is nothing
And
There can be nothing.

88. GRACE AND EFFORT

Effort tells me openly:
God-realisation
Is a most difficult task.

Grace tells me secretly:
God-realisation
Is a task not so difficult to perform.

89. WHY NOT?

Why not
Ask for more,
O incapacity-ant?

Why not
Ask for less,
O capacity-lion?

90. GOD COULD NOT RECOGNISE ME

With a beggar's humility
I came to God.
He could not recognise me.

With a prince's pride
I came to God.
He could not recognise me then, either.

91. HE WILL SOON BE NEEDED

He was once needed
By incapacity-doubt.

He is now needed
By capacity-faith.

He will soon be needed
By God's supreme Satisfaction-Perfection-Light.

92. O FOUNTAIN OF SURRENDER-LIGHT

O fountain of thought,
You are so beautiful.

O fountain of will,
You are so truthful.

O fountain of surrender-light,
You are so fruitful.

93. HOPE IS NO MORE SWEET

Alas, the pangs of teeming hopes
Are torturing me, my all.
Hope is no more sweet.
Hope is bitter frustration-failure.

94. BIRTH AND DEATH

The birth of human doubt
Is the death of divine faith.

The birth of divine faith
Is Immortality's perfect Manifestation-light.

95. RUN AWAY IMMEDIATELY

Do you need earth's constant love?
Then run away immediately
From your jealousy-mountain.

Do you want Heaven's constant love?
Then run away immediately
From your insecurity-cave.

96. I HAVE PLANTED A SMILE

I have planted a smile
In humanity's heart.
I am sure one day
It will grow and illumine
Ignorance-world,
And fulfil and satisfy
Wisdom-world.

97. THE PRICE OF EXPERIENCE

The price of earth-experience
I have paid:
Therefore
I am totally free from earth.

The price of Heaven-realisation
I have not yet paid;
Therefore
I am helplessly bound to Heaven.

98. O ENSLAVED HUMANITY

O enslaved humanity,
My heart's oneness
Really suffers for you.

O enraptured divinity,
My life's sincerity
Really rejoices in your delight-sea.

99. SACRIFICING LIFE OF MAN

Expanding eye of man
Is good.

Illumining heart of man
Is better.

Sacrificing life of man
Is by far the best.

100. THE EXILES

Yesterday
His insincerity was exiled
From the face of light.

Today
His impurity is exiled
From the heart of light.

Tomorrow
His insecurity will be exiled
From the life of light.

101. AT LONG LAST

At long last I have come to know who I am.
I am humanity's success-life
And
Divinity's progress-soul.

102. MY HEART'S SACRED FLAMES

My tears
Are my heart's sacred flames.
These flames
Help me see
God the eternal Sun
And help me feed
Man the eternal preparation.

103. REAL HOPE-FLAME

Real hope-flame is not swift.
It is slow.
It is steady.
It is certain.
It is the illumining harbinger
Of real Reality-Day.

104. MY LIFE IS DANCING AND SINGING

My life
Has broken open all its limits.
It is now dancing the dance
Of earth's success-pride
And
Singing the song
Of Heaven's progress-light.

105. O MY EMPTY HEART

O my empty heart,
Do not cry!
God is coming.
True, He is taking time,
But I assure you
This time when He comes
Your constant love for Him
Shall make Him delighted to be back.

106. BECAUSE I LOVE

Because
I love this mortal life,
I love this precarious world-night.

Because
I shall love that immortal life,
I shall love that precious Heaven-light.

107. I WILL LOVE DEATH

I know I will love death.
Why?
Because death too
Is God's creation
And because death reminds me
Of the existence of her sister:
Infinity's Life immortal.

108. MY FAILURE-LIFE

The tear-garland of my failure-life
I place at Your Feet,
O Lord Supreme.
It is painful, yet soulful.
It is soulful, therefore fruitful.

109. BE READY

Be ready to fly, my body.
You will enjoy flying
Like your big brother, soul,
In the silence-vision of Heaven.

Be ready to walk, my soul.
You will enjoy walking
Like your little brother, body,
In the sound-reality of earth.

110. LEAVE ALL BEHIND YOU

Leave all behind you.
There is nothing,
Absolutely nothing
For you to carry
God wants to see you –
You, only you.
He is tired of seeing
Everybody else
And
Everything else.

111. YOUR NAME

Your name
Was declared unexpectedly
In the heart-cry of the morning sky;
Therefore, stay a little longer on earth.

Your name
Will be declared unmistakably
In the soul-smile of the evening sky
By God Himself.

112. DO NOT WAIT FOR EARTH

My soul,
Do not wait for earth.
Go on!
Earth is too slow.
Go on!
Earth is too uncertain.
Go on!
Earth is too suspicious.
Go on!
Earth is too ignorant.
Go on!

113. WHO WANTS?

Who wants a sound-life?
I do.
Why?
Because the sound-life
Is really something astonishing.

Who wants a silence-life?
I do.
Why?
Because the silence-life
Is really something enlightening.

114. FOREVER AND NOW

No difference
Between
Forever and now.
What is forever?
Forever is composed of
All-spreading
And
All-fulfilling
Nows.

115. HOW ABOUT A NEW STYLE

Lord, how about a new style
In Your Compassion-Heart?
So far Your Compassion-Heart
Has been unreserved.
Can You not try to make it
Unconditional, too?
Try, Lord.
I assure You,
You will succeed.

116. A DAY WITHOUT MEDITATION

A day without meditation
Is self-deception-night.

A day without meditation
Is self-destruction-fight.

A day without meditation
Is reality-negation flight.

117. TEN YEARS OF INTENSE ASPIRATION

Ten years of intense aspiration
Made him see the present God
Who wants from him
His own Manifestation on earth.
He said to God:
"Lord, I am really surprised
To see that You too need something.
Anyway, I assure You,
I shall not forget to do You the favour."

118. YOU SHOULD LEAVE ME

Insincerity, if you do not leave me,
I shall leave you
Mercilessly,
Therefore
You should leave me
Graciously.

Insecurity, if you do not leave me,
I shall leave you
Immediately,
Therefore
You should leave me
Cleverly.

119. I HAVE A NEW FRIEND

To make a very long story
Very short,
I wish to tell you
I have now a new friend,
  a real friend,
Unlike all my previous friends.
Do you want to know
My best and only real friend's name?
Hope-flame.

120. DON'T TAKE YOUR LIFE TOO SERIOUSLY

Don't take your life
Too seriously.
There should be
Some amusement
To free us from confusion-tension
In the mind-jungle.
It is necessary.
You will feel it
And
You will believe it,
I assure you.

121. HERE WE ARE AGAIN

Here we are on earth again.
God says to me,
"Son, be brave enough to please Me
This time."

Here we are in Heaven again.
I say to God,
"Father, be kind enough to leave me alone
This time
And
For all time."

122. NOT ONE, BUT MANY

Not one failure
But many
When I run after
The desire-train.

Not one success
But many
When I sit down
For good
At the foot of aspiration's mountain-smile.

123. I ENTERTAIN BY MYSELF

I entertain all by myself.
It is really great.
I do not want anyone
To accompany me.
Not even You, Lord,
For Your presence is too expensive.
I really have run short of funds.
I mean, my aspiration-funds.

124. THE THINGS I NEED

These are the things that I actually need:
I need hope-plant to grow in me;
I need satisfaction-tree to stand before me;
I need perfection-sun always to love me.

125. JUST TO SEE

Just to see
If my stupidity-friend was here on earth
I came all the way to earth
From Heaven.

Just to see
If my wisdom-friend is there in Heaven
I shall go all the way from earth
To Heaven.

126. EXACTLY WHAT I NEED

This is exactly what I need:
A perfection-life
In my Eternity's sound-sea
And
In my Eternity's silence-sky.

127. IT HURTS ME

It hurts me a little,
Lord, when the world speaks ill of You.
But it hurts me a lot,
Lord, when I speak ill of You;
For You are so beautiful to look at,
You are so delicious to eat,
You are so precious to possess
That I really do not know what to do.
I am not only useless but helpless.

128. ASK GOD!

Ask God!
He will tell you
How divinely beautiful you are,
Since you have decided
Not to believe me.

Ask God!
He will tell you
How supremely fruitful you are,
Since you have decided
Not to believe me.

129. I LOVE MYSELF

I love myself.
At least that much
I can do for myself
Without anybody's help.
Am I not really great?
I am sure I really am.

130. EASIER DONE THAN SAID

What is easier done
Than said?
To grow God-satisfaction-tree
In my heart's gratitude garden.

131. MAKE UP YOUR MIND, LORD

Make up Your mind, Lord.
Do You want to love me?
Make up Your mind.
I am giving You the first choice.
I hate to remain any longer
Mean to You.
Today I declare my real name:
Heart's magnanimity.

132. DO STAY WITH ME HERE

So You have finally come,
My old friend, God.
This time I shall not
Let You go.
Without You I feel
I am insecurity incarnate on earth.
If You really want me to work for You,
Then do stay with me here
All the time.

133. SINCERITY AND PURITY

What is in your mind?
Sincerity?
May I just glance at it?

What is in your heart?
Purity?
May I just glance at it?

It is your sincerity-mind
That has made you great.
It is your purity-heart
That has made you good.

134. THEY WILL HELP YOU

Your soul will help you
To see God.
Stay in your soul.

Your God will help you
To love your soul.
Stay in your God.

135. A MESSAGE FOR YOUR MIND

A message for your mind:
One day your mind
Will forget to desert God-Love:
One day your mind
Will remember to assert God-Compassion.

136. I SHALL WAIT UNTIL YOU CALL

I shall wait until You call.
But please call me soon.
I have so much to say to You.
I have so much to learn from You.
I have so much to unlearn
By the touch of Your Forgiveness-Feet.

137. THE COMPANIONS OF SINCERITY

These are the companions of sincerity:
Simplicity-child
Security-lion
Purity-flower
Satisfaction-tree.

138. EVERYTHING CHANGES

Everything changes.
Nothing remains unchanged,
Not even God's Compassion-Height
And
Man's suspicion-night.

139. USE YOUR WILL-POWER

Use your will-power.
In your mind
You will realise
Your greatness-height;
In your heart
You will realise
Your goodness-light.

140. WHEN I DIE

What will happen to me
When I die?
Heaven will not care for
My heart's excruciating pangs.
Earth will not care for
My soul's all-illumining delight.

141. FAITH AND WILL-POWER

Faith and will-power,
Essentially the same.
Faith tells me:
I shall do everything for you
At God's choice Hour.
Will-power says to me:
I have already done everything for you,
For God's Hour has already struck.

142. NOW OR NEVER!

Do it now or never!
Realise God.
Once you have
Realised God
Time bows to you,
Truth teaches you,
Satisfaction-perfection
Becomes all yours.

143. EXCEPT ONE THING

Do something, do anything
Except one thing:
Don't think and feel
That you are another
Experience-God
And
Realisation-man.

144. LET US QUITE OFTEN MEET

Faith,
Let us quite often meet.
You tell me
How to love and adore God.
I shall tell you
How to become another God.

145. HE MEDITATED UPON A DEWDROP

He meditated
Upon a dewdrop
And became
God-Humility's perfection-soul,
God-Reality's satisfaction-goal.

146. EACH SONG IS A FLAME

Each soulful song is a flame
In the aspiring heart.
Where is that heart?
It is in the supreme art
Of constant self-giving.

147. THE VISION

The vision of the poet
I had.

The vision of the artist
I have.

The vision of the Yogi
I shall eternally have.

148. GIVE ME THREE THINGS MORE

Give me three things more
And then I shall really
Be satisfied.
Now I tell you
What they are:
Realisation-oneness,
Revelation-perfection,
Satisfaction-smile.

149. YOU HAVE YET MUCH TO DO

Do not leave,
Do not withdraw.
You have yet much to give,
You have yet much to learn.

What are you going to give?
Your heart's tears.
What are you going to learn?
Your soul's smile.

150. WHERE IS PEACE?

Humanity needs peace.
But where is peace?
It is in love.
Where is love?
It is in life-acceptance
And
Self-transcendence.

151. O DEAR ONES

O sweet inspiration,
I always need you.

O pure aspiration,
I always love you.

O brave realisation,
I and my life
Totally and unconditionally
Surrender to you,
And you alone.

152. THE WORLD OF THOUGHT, THE WORLD OF WILL

He went back
Into the world of thought
Only to be ridiculed and humiliated.

Yet he cared not to come back
Into the world of will,
For he cared more for intellect-spears
Than for love-shield.

153. HE WAS HAPPY THREE TIMES

He was happy only three times
In his entire life:
Once when he helped a climbing man,
Once when he saved a falling man,
Once when he became one with a dying man.

154. SIN

Forgiveness of teeming sins
Is good.

Illumination of teeming sins
Is better.

Not to resort at any time to sin
Is by far the best.

155. HE WAS CONSUMED BY FIRE

He was consumed
By the burning fire
Of thought-world.
He can only be revived
By the contemplation-power
Of God's all-immortalising faith-world.

156. MODERN SCIENCE

Frustrated, he says,
"Modern science is the topmost branch
Of death-tree."

Satisfied, he says,
"Modern science will be the root
Of life's immortality-discovery."

157. DON'T MIX WITH HIM

Don't mix with him.
He is a blind human fool.

Don't mix with him.
He is a clever human rogue.

Don't mix with him.
He has built a world of fruitless fantasy
All around him.

158. A GREAT RUNNER

He was a great runner.
In the outer world he ran
To satisfy his quenchless thirst
For name and fame.
In the inner world he ran
To feed and satisfy
The God-hunger in him.

159. AS THE EARTH TURNS

As the earth turns away from the sun,
Even so
His stupidity has turned him away
From God's Compassion-Day
And
Man's unalloyed affection-light,
   oneness-delight.

160. THEREFORE I AM HAPPY

I bow and obey;
Therefore I am happy.

I do not want to escape,
I want to accept and embrace;
Therefore I am happy.

My gratitude-heart for God
Is not accustomed to death;
Therefore I am happy.

161. TODAY'S BASE FEAR

Today's base fear
Becomes guilt tomorrow.
Tomorrow's guilty consciousness
Becomes the destruction-volcano
For the years to come.

162. IN RENUNCIATION-LIGHT

He lives inside
The circle of his golden silence,
The mask of ignorance no more near him.
He has totally discarded it.
He has also shunned his zenith-glory.
In renunciation-light he is enjoying
The Delight Supreme.

163. THE AGE OF ACHIEVEMENT

This is not the age of triumph.
This is the age of sacrifice.
This is the age of service.
This is the age of love-achievement,
   truth-achievement
   and
   perfection-achievement,
Here, there, everywhere.

164. ANGELIC GRACE

Do you want to dance with angelic grace?
Then cry in the inner world.

Do you want to sing with an angelic voice?
Then live in the inner world.

Do you want to treasure angelic grace?
Then smile in the Silence of all silences.

165. HE DEDICATES HIS LIFE

His frustration-life
He has dedicated
To his old friend,
Death.

His dedication-life
He now dedicates
To his new and eternal friend,
Immortality-life.

166. HE HAS NOT SURRENDERED

Although his life was marked by failure,
He did not surrender to ignorance-night.

Although he was drunk with fatigue,
　excruciating fatigue,
He did not surrender to ignorance-night.

Although wild tears have conquered his life,
　inner and outer,
He has not surrendered to ignorance-night.

His is not the nature to surrender,
But to accept life
And brave the buffets of life
And thus come out victorious.

167. TWO THINGS HE TREASURES

Two things he always treasures:
The invisible wings
Of his heart's silence-bird
And
The visible arms
Of his body's dedication-life.

168. THE HUMAN MIND

The human mind
Is but a foolish wind.

The human mind
Is but a foolish monkey.

The human mind
Is but a foolish expanse.

The human mind
Is but a foolish sigh of disbelief.

169. A QUESTION STILL UNANSWERED

O Lord,
Do take me beyond the reach of desire.

O Lord,
Do place me within the reach of aspiration.

O Lord,
One question of my mind yet remains
   unanswered:
Will I ever love You devotedly,
   soulfully,
   unreservedly
   and
   unconditionally,
Ever?

170. THE INNER MAN

The inner man is paid
When the outer man sees and receives.

The inner man is happy
When the outer man achieves and becomes.

The inner man knows the secret
Of God's Vision-Illumination
And
God's Reality-Perfection.

171. O INSECURITY

O insecurity,
I have saved you.
I have saved your doomed, grieved body.

O insecurity,
I have given you sincere happiness.
I have made you the instrument of Heaven.
Otherwise, you would have remained
The instrument of hell.

172. DOUBT IS AN INSTRUMENT

Doubt is an instrument
Of perpetuating hell.

Doubt is an instrument
Of temptation-frustration.

Doubt is an instrument
Of destruction-realisation.

173. MAN IS NOT A GOD

Why is man not a god?
Man is not a god because
Man is afraid of God-Responsibility
And God's all-pervading Duty
And God's universal Oneness-Reality.

174. NOW HE COMPETES WITH DEATH

Before he made friends with aspiration-life
He was the friend of death.
Now he competes with death
And its friends:
Fear, anxiety and doubt.
In himself he sees the seeds
Of world-transforming God-Smile.

175. I LOVE THE CHILDREN OF GOD

I love the crying children of God
Because they are pure.
I love the waiting children of God
Because they are sure.

176. A LIFE OF PRISON-HOPE

He lives in a prison-home
Of stubborn inconscience.
He hides in the cave
Of insecurity
And tries to escape
From the tight embrace of the past.
Alas, his is a life
Of prison-hope.

177. TWO LESSONS OF LIFE

Two significant lessons of life
He has learned
From life itself:
To love the human life
In the life divine;
And
To transform the animal into the human
For the divine to play its most significant role
In the human life.

178. A MERE GLANCE

Just a mere glance of the Lord
Can erase the music
Of his inhuman life.
Just a mere glance of the Lord!

179. HIS FEAR WON

His fear fought
With his desire.
His fear won.

His Immortality-breath fought
With his mortality-life.
His mortality-life won.

180. IMMORTALITY

Infinity
Is a gift from above.
Eternity
Is a gift from above.
Divinity
Is a gift from above.
But Immortality
Is an achievement here on earth.

181. YOU WILL BE HAPPY

Be indifferent to blame and praise.
You will be happy.

Don't be sick of solitude.
You will be happy.

Discard the splendour of desire.
You will be happy.

Recognise not the ranklings of jealousy.
You will be happy.

Let death be inaugurated in your vital's
 volcano-pride.
You will be happy.

182. HE IS A FOOL

He is a fool.
He lives in his determination-doubt.

He is a fool.
He forgets to treasure his surrendering breath.

He is a fool.
He tries to define
His ascending love of God
   and
God's descending love of him.

183. YOU ARE A TRUE HERO

You are a true hero.
I need your life's
Surrender-strength to God.
I need your life's
Satisfaction-perfection
In God's operation
In and through you.

184. NOW THAT I KNOW

Now that I know where joy is
I shall no longer
Act like a fool.
Joy is in the vision-light
Of non-expectation.

185. EACH CRY IS A VISION

Each cry is a vision.
Each vision is a realisation.
Each realisation is a perfection.
Each perfection is God's Satisfaction in man
And
Man's transcendence-delight in God.

186. A NEW TONIC

I am indeed a part of you,
Therefore
Do not be afraid of me,
My poor doubt.
From today I shall serve you
With a new tonic:
Oneness-light.

187. EACH THOUGHT IS A PRAYER

Each thought is a prayer.
Each prayer is a satisfaction.
Each satisfaction
Is God in preparation
For His own Self-transcendence.

188. AN ACHIEVEMENT UNPARALLELED

Heaven's pride
Garlands your golden life-boat,
Not because you have reached
The shore
But because you have left
The starting point.
Indeed, this is an achievement unparalleled.

189. GOD NEEDS YOUR HEART

Your heart is all false,
Counterfeit.
I do not need it.
But alas, God needs it.
Why?
God needs it
Because you try and cry
And cry and try
To love God,
Although in your own way.
No harm, that is what
Everybody does in the beginning.

190. A PURE HEART SEES

What does a pure heart do?
A pure heart sees
That God is its Eternity's Friend,
God is its Infinity's Smile,
God is its Immortality's Reality.

191. WHERE ARE YOU SLEEPING, PURITY?

Where are you sleeping, purity?
There is a room in my heart.
Do try it.
If it pleases you
I shall give it to you free.
I promise a hundred times.

192. A SOUL-LIFE OF GRATITUDE

A soul-life of gratitude
To You I offer,
My Master-Lord,
For Your satisfaction
In my service-love-boat.

193. THERE AND HERE

I am there
And
I am here.

I am there
In Heaven
To sing God's Vision-Song,
An easy song.

I am here
On earth
To play God's Game,
A difficult game.

194. MAN'S MONKEY MIND

Man's mind has no
Fixed rule
And
It can never have one,
For it does not sincerely desire
To come out of its restless
Monkey-incarnation.

195. SON, I FORGIVE YOU

Lord, do You forgive me
When I do everything wrong?

"Son, I forgive you."

Why?

"Because you are asking the right person.
I am the only one
Who can and will forgive you."

196. THE CHILDREN CRY

Children of the heart
Cry with the desire
To offer their love-light to the world.

Children of the mind
Cry with the desire
To receive the thought-might from the world.

197. A DEBT TO PAY

I have a debt to pay
To my Earth-Mother:
Service-life.

I have a debt to pay
To my Heaven-Father:
Love-smile.

198. THE BEGINNING AND THE END

His soulful beginning
Has found its fruitful end.
Where?
Where the beginning
And the end
Each other need
For God-Satisfaction
And
Man-perfection.

199. SOARING AND SINGING

Soaring and singing,
His soul-vision came to me.

Crying and dying,
My earth-reality is running towards him.

200. SOW AND GROW

Sow
Conviction-seed.

Grow
Perfection-plant.

Become
Satisfaction-fruit.

201. POOR JEALOUSY

Poor jealousy!
Forgive her,
She is living in the wrong home:
Mind-insecurity.

If she wants to live
In the heart,
Then the heart will give her
Its magnanimity-light.

202. THE SIGN OF A GOD-HEART

To cry
For earth-pleasure
Is the sign of a little heart.

To smile
At earth-frustration
Is the sign of a big heart.

To surrender
And then cry or smile
As soul-necessity demands
Is the sign of a God-Heart.

203. WISDOM

Cave-wisdom:
Renounce!

Palace-wisdom:
Announce!

God-wisdom:
Accept,
Transform
And
Together smile!

204. THE MOUNTAIN-SMILE

The mountain-smile
Is a smile
In which you see
The height
Transcending its own heights,
The illumination
Transcending its own illuminations.

205. I SHALL SMILE

When my dry logic dies,
I shall secretly smile.

When the philosopher in me
Surrenders to the seeker in me,
I shall openly smile.

206. INSIDE HIS SMILE

He smiled
And gave me the answer
To my life's query.

Inside his smile
I saw only one thing:
"I, too, eternally need you."

207. DON'T SPEAK SO LOUDLY

Don't speak so loudly
Or all the world will know it,
And it will laugh at you.

Don't speak so lifelessly,
Or all the world will know it,
And it will laugh at you.

Just speak confidently, smilingly.
Lo, the world is loving you
And needing you,
You alone.

208. HE CAME, HE LEFT

He came
Because
He needed
Earth-tears
To be dynamically brave.

He left
Because
He needed
Heaven-smiles
To be soulfully beautiful.

209. LORD, DO TEACH ME!

Lord, I do not know.
Do teach me!

"Son, first unlearn
What you have so far learned.
I shall then
Not only teach you
But also make you another God like Me."

210. EARTH-NAME, HEAVEN-NAME

My earth-name
Is Heaven's necessity-reality.

My Heaven-name
Is earth's responsibility-reality
And
Earth's surrender-divinity.

211. YOU, TOO, HAVE A PLACE

You are the doubter
And
The teeming doubts;
Therefore
Nobody needs you.
But I love you
Because you too
Have a place at God's Feet
To sing your transformation-song.

212. WHEN

O my earth, when will you smile?
O my Heaven, when will you cry?
O my God, when will You appear?

When earth smiles,
I see.
When Heaven cries,
I feel.
When God appears,
I become.

213. AGAIN AND AGAIN

I shall come here
Again and again
To love God's Feet of Light
Because
They are Compassion-Beauty,
They are Perfection-Reality.

214. WHEN I FEEL THE PULL

When I feel the pull
Of desire
My weak vital surrenders
To nothingness black.

When I feel the pull
Of aspiration
My strong heart surrenders
To oneness white.

215. YOU TRUST ME

You trust me, don't you?
I assure you,
I shall never fail you.

I trust myself, don't I?
If I do not
Then I shall start right now,
For my sanity's beauty.

216. I AM DYING

Lord, save me,
I am dying.

"Son, smile!
I, too, am dying
With you
And
For you."

217. THE REALISATION OF LIFE'S MISTAKES

The realisation
Of life's mistakes
Is painful
But unavoidable.
Today you realise
Your follies;
Tomorrow you will realise
That perfection is what
You wanted
And perfection is what
You undoubtedly have.

218. HIS COMPASSION-SMILE

His Compassion-smile
Tells me
He can give me unconditionally
And
I can receive Him unreservedly.

219. WHEN YOU SCOLD ME

When you scold me
I love you infinitely more,
Because
At that time you feel
That I can after all
Become something really good,
   divine,
    supreme
     and perfect.

220. PURITY

Purity: a thought-light
That shakes mankind,
Transforms mankind,
Glorifies mankind
And
Fulfils God in God's own Way.

221. NOW THE TRUTH-SECRET IS OUT

Now the truth-secret is out:
God really needs me.

Now the truth-secret is out:
God's satisfaction entirely depends
On my oneness-height with Him.

222. WHERE HAVE YOU BEEN?

O Lord, where have You been?
I have not seen You
For a long time.

"But son, I have all along
Seen you."

Where?

"In your self-imposed insecurity."

223. THE GIVER

You give joy to all;
Therefore
You are great.

You give love to all;
Therefore
You are good.

You give God to all;
Therefore
You are another God,
At least to me.

224. HE PROMISED TO RETURN

He promised to return
And he will:
Not with compassion
Like last time
But
With a sword
For world-redemption.

225. WHEN YOU INSULT ME

When you insult me
I love you infinitely more,
Because
I know then that
You need my service:
Perfection-service,
Of course.

226. BEGINNING AND CONCLUSION

Your beginning was precarious.
Your conclusion will be
   precious,
   prosperous,
   gracious.

227. EXPERIENCE-GAIN

There is no loss:
It is all experience-gain.
Believe it or not,
You will realise it is true
Long before you start
Consciously sailing
In God's Self-Transcendence Boat.

228. WHAT DOES AMERICA HAVE?

What does America have?
It has everything
Except one thing:
Relaxation-taste
In perfection-test.

229. THE COURAGE TO TRY

When you have
The courage to try,
You have everything,
For God-revealing Reality
Loves you
And
Needs you.

230. GOD-POWER

Faith-power
I use to achieve.

Love-power
I use to become.

God-power
I use to surrender.
To whom?
God the Compassion-Height
  and
God the Perfection-Light.

231. O WALLS OF HISTORY

O walls of history,
Let me pass through you.
I shall see only
The truth in you.
I shall distribute only
The delicious reality-sweets of you
To the world around me.

232. THE CHILDREN LOVE HIM

The children of the West
Love him
Because he talks about God.

The children of the East
Love him
Because he knows God.

233. GOD-LOVE, SELF-LOVE

I love God
Because
He is great and good.

I love myself
Because
I need God,
And nobody else.
Never!

234. WHEN HE APPEARS

When
He appears
Everything clears up.

When
He appears
Everybody cheers up.

When
He appears
Everybody nears not only the Goal
But the Goal-Beauty itself.

235. DO NOT GIVE UP!

Happy days are yet to come.
Do not give up!

Happier days are bound to come.
Do not give up!

Happiest days will be fast approaching you.
Do not give up!

236. TO CONQUER, TO WIN

To conquer the night
What I need
Is my soul's light-power.

To win the day
What I need
Is my life's dedication-power.

237. I LOVE YOUR HEART-BEAUTY'S CRY

Dear America,
I love
Your heart-beauty's cry
Because it needs me.
And I need it, too!
It needs me openly
And
I need it unmistakably.

238. DO YOU NEED ME?

I do not know
What to say to you.
You have been so kind to me.
Do tell me one thing:
Do you need me?
"I need you and I shall always need you
Because your need of me
Is well-founded and well-informed."

239. EXCEPT ONE THING

Nothing
Is boring
Except one thing:
Incapacity.

Nothing
Is soaring
Except one thing:
Satisfaction-necessity.

240. GOD'S ONENESS

God's greatness
Puzzles me.

God's goodness
Fascinates me.

God's oneness
Satisfies me
And
Glorifies me.

241. I NEED GOD

I like God.
He is so kind to me.

I love God.
He is so blind to me.

I need God.
He is so real to me.

242. THE REAL IN MYSELF

At last I submit
To the real in myself.
What is the real in myself?
My love-world's
Oneness-delight
With God.

243. THE BEAUTY OF MY DREAM

The beauty of my dream tells me,
"Seeker, I have come
To love you.
You are only of God
And
You are only for God."

244. MIND'S EYE, HEART'S EYE

In his mind's eye
There is no reality
In God's Creation-Breath.

In his heart's eye
There is nothing
And
There can be nothing
Save and except reality all-where.

245. HEART'S ECSTASY-FLOOD

Not to love God
Is the pain of the heart.

To love God
And to make God feel
He is loved and needed
Always and always
Is the ecstasy-flood of the heart.

246. O SLEEPLESS SOUL

O sleepless soul,
Because you are brave
You are great,
Because you are sincere
You are good,
Because you so unreservedly give
You are perfect,
Absolutely perfect.

247. THE BEST

Poise,
You are the best of me.

Purity,
You are the best in me.

Perfection,
You are the best for me.

248. DARK THOUGHTS HAVE RETURNED

Former dark thoughts have returned;
Therefore
I am dying in grief
And
I am crying to end the noise-wheel
Of creation-satisfaction.

249. FEAR AND DOUBT

Fear frightens me.
What is fear?
A self-imposed torture.

Doubt devours me.
What is doubt?
An unconscious destruction-poison.

250. UNWILLING

You are
Unwilling to be fed
By God.

He is
Unwilling to be fed
By God.

I am
Unwilling to be seen
By God's Justice-light
But
I am
Eagerly longing to be seen
By God's Compassion-Might.

251. WHO WRITES HIS DREAMS?

Who writes his dreams?
God the Creator.

Who publishes his dreams?
God the Preserver.

Who distributes his dreams?
God the Fulfiller,
God the eternal Lover.

252. MY LIFE'S SONG

O Lord, in Your Heart's Joy
My life's song begins,
And in my heart's suffering
My life's song ends.

253. DESPAIR IS STRONG

Despair is not weak;
It is strong.
It fights against our hope.
It fights against our determination.
It fights even against our heart's
   conviction-light.

254. AFRAID TO FIGHT?

Afraid to fight?
How then are you going to win
In the battlefield of life?

Afraid to fight?
How then are you going to wear
The garland of victory?

Afraid to fight?
How then can God-Perfection manifest itself
In and through you
In the battlefield of life?

Be not afraid to fight!
Fight for Truth and surrender to Truth alone.

255. HIS LIFE IS APPRECIATED

His complete simplicity-life
Is appreciated by all his dear ones.

His complete sincerity-life
Is appreciated by all those who know him.

His complete purity-life
Is loved by all those who need
An iota of purity-breath.

256. O NEVER-WORKING BODY

O never-resting mind,
Do take rest for some time,
For you really need some rest.
O never-working body,
Do work for some time at least.
You do need to work.
You have rested beyond your necessity's
  satisfaction.
Be active!
Rest no more!
Sit for the test of life!
Manifest God-Beauty in and through yourself!

257. DON'T THINK OF THE PAST!

Don't think of the past!
You will be forced to enter
Into the chaos of thought.
You will be forced to enter
Into the chaos of passion.
You will be forced to enter
Into the dust of lifetimes.
You will be forced to play the role
Of Eternity's most deplorable beggar.

258. THE PATH OF SATISFACTION-LIGHT

Begging is not good.
Asking is not good.
Demanding is not good.
Then what is good?
Loving and becoming the Oneness-Reality
For the path of satisfaction-light
Is good, always good.

259. CHERISHED DREAM AND CHERISHED REALITY

I always cherish a dream
And that dream is the dream
Of self-determination.

I always cherish a reality
And that reality is the reality
Of God-manifestation.

260. GOD DANCED AND DANCED

When my mind's innocence and my mind's virtue
Met together
God danced and danced and danced.
He completely forgot
How to walk any more,
How to run any more;
He only danced and danced.

261. JOY IS MY NAME

Joy was my name
When I thought that I loved God
More than anybody else.

Joy is my name
When I think that God loves me
More than He loves anybody else.

Joy shall be my name
When I can think that God's Love-distribution
Is for God to decide
And not for my human longing.

262. AN INNOCENT TEAR-DROP

An innocent tear-drop of humanity
Killed me.

An infant fear-drop of humanity
Killed my heart.

A fraction of a doubt-smile of humanity
Killed my life.

263. YOU LIVE FOR ME

My Lord,
In exchange for the tears of my sorrow
You have given me Your loving
And living Presence.

My Lord,
You live not for Yourself
But You live for my life's satisfaction-smile
In the tears of my ever-climbing heart.

264. THE HEART OF SORROW

His is the heart of sorrow.
His is the heart of tears.
He longs to learn the oblivion-song.
Alas, his life-boat is tied to the coast of doleful life.

265. THE OTHER SHORE OF LIFE

The other shore of life
Is beautiful.
Who says so?
The dissatisfied vital.

The other shore of life
Is meaningful.
Who says so?
The intelligent mind.

The other shore of life
Is perfection-satisfaction.
Who says so?
The doubter-hater of this shore.

266. EXPLORE

Explore your mind.
There is much that you will be able to discover.
Explore your vital.
It needs transformation through purification.

267. HIS DAYS SLIP BY

All his days slip by
In lethargy-black.
All his days slip by
In incapacity-brown.
All his promise-joy slips by
In oblivion-swoon.
Yet he cherishes the expectancy
Of God's arrival.

268. GRACE

Sincerity cures all disgrace.
Purity revives all Grace.
Humility immediately adds to Grace.
Surrender to God-Will immortalises all Grace.

269. THE BEST THING TO DO

To doubt God's existence
Is a fatal flaw.

To doubt one's own existence
Is an unforgivable flaw.

To love oneself divinely
Is a real thing to do.

To love God before one loves oneself
Is by far the best thing to do.

270. DESIRE-LIFE, ASPIRATION-LIFE

Desire-life still cries in you.
You want to know
What you can do?
You can love your aspiration-life
Infinitely more.
Desire-life will become jealous
Of your aspiration-life
And will leave you once and for all.

271. A THOUSAND SIGHS

It is a thousand sighs
That break the promise-light
Of our divinity's beauty
And necessity's magnanimity.

272. GOD'S PRIDE

Who was God's pride?
The searching man.

Who is God's pride?
The crying man.

Who will be God's pride?
The cheerfully surrendering man.

273. THE VICEROY IN ME

Human reason's viceroy is in me;
Its name is justice.
Divine compassion's viceroy is in me;
Its name is truth-climbing progress.

274. THE RUNNERS

I run to death
Unafraid.

Death runs to me
Unconcerned.

God runs to me
Smilingly.

God runs to death
Tyrannically.

275. THREE STEPS TO GREATNESS

Three steps to greatness:
He loves the world's helplessness.
He becomes the world's sincerity.
He sacrifices all his light
For all the world's stupidity.

276. BEAUTY, RESPONSIBILITY AND NECESSITY

Beauty: the heart
Of humanity.

Responsibility: the soul
Of divinity.

Necessity: the life
Of Immortality.

277. I SHALL END MY LIFE-SONG

I shall end my life-song
With a million sighs
Unfulfilled,
Unappreciated
And
Even unheard.

278. TWO THINGS I NEED

Two things I always need:
The consolation of my imagination
And
The manifestation of God's Compassion.

279. COMPASSION AND PERFECTION

Divine Compassion: what is it?
The sanctuary of human incapacity.

Divine Perfection: what is it?
The dream-reality of God-Capacity.

280. YOU MUST BECOME

You must live,
Therefore
You must love.

You must love,
Therefore
You must become.

You must become.
Why?
To please God and His oneness with you.

281. HEAR ME!

Hear me!
I shall break
Your stupidity-casket
And
Your divinity's satisfaction-door.

282. EVERYONE IS GOOD

Everyone is good,
Including the animal in me.
Why?
Because it admires the human in me.

Everyone is good,
Including the human in me.
Why?
Because it feels a conscious need
Of the divine in God.

283. SURRENDER-LIFE

Love-life never dies.
Devotion-life ever lives.
Surrender-life transcends
Both death and life.
It lives in the heart
Of beginningless silence
And
Endless sound.

284. CONSOLATION

He sat at the foot of the sky
For consolation.

He sat in the heart of the sky
For consolation.

He sat on the top of the sky
For consolation.

No consolation!
At last he made his conscious oneness
With God-life perfect.
In his service-light he received
Not only consolation-illumination
But perfection-satisfaction
of the transcendental Heights.

285. CONFESSION

Confession, if it is reluctant,
Is worse than useless.

Confession, if it is forced,
Is worse than useless.

Confession spontaneous, the self-giving reality,
Is better than the best.

286. HIS LIFE ON EARTH

His very life on earth
Is the soul of discipline-light.

His very heart on earth
Is the smile of perfection-height.

His very body on earth
Is the singleness of God's living Purpose
Here on earth.

287. YOU ARE REALLY GREAT

Your intuition-mind
Is really great.
Your sacrifice-heart
Is really great.
Your perfection-concern
Is really great.
Your oneness-life with the world at large
Is really great.

288. MY COMRADE ETERNAL

I do not doubt;
Therefore
My Master is my comrade eternal.

I do not fear;
Therefore
My Master and my boat
Easily take me to the shores
Of the ever-transcending Beyond.

289. DO YOU KNOW?

Humility,
Do you know that
You are always safe?

Purity,
Do you know that
You are in God's very Heart?

Sincerity,
Do you know that
Through you
God the Eternal Dreamer
And
God the Eternal Fulfiller
Sees?

290. THOSE WHO NEVER SLEEP

Many are there
Who sleep too much.
Very few are there
Who do not sleep enough.
Again, there are those
Who never sleep at all.
Theirs is the continuous search
For God-oneness,
For God-perfection,
For Eternity's God-embrace.

291. O LIGHT OF COMPASSION

O Light of Compassion,
Your miracle-breath
Is spreading smiling fragrance.
Tomorrow without fail
I shall win the tug-of-war
Against ignorance-night.
Why?
Just because today You have claimed me
As Your very own;
Just because today I have claimed You
As my very own,
O Light of Compassion.

292. GIANT HEART, GIANT EYE

Earth has a giant heart.
It can tolerate everything,
It can assimilate everything.

Heaven has a giant eye.
It can see everything,
It can purify everything,
It can enlighten everything.

293. DON'T SAIL IN THE DOUBT-BOAT

Don't sail
In the doubt-boat.
If you do, you are bound
To reach the soundless shore.

Don't sail
In the doubt-boat.
If you do, you are bound
To meet with nadir-darkness
And slumbering inconscience-cry.

294. GOD REALLY LOVES YOU

Do not argue with God.
He really loves you.

Do not criticise God.
He really loves you.

Set aside your pride.
Lo, God has set you free.

295. DO NOT SLAY YOURSELF

Do not slay yourself.
Do not kill yourself.
Your Lord will not only save you
But illumine and immortalise you.

Do not slay yourself.
Do not kill yourself.
Your Lord has given you your life.
Your body and soul are of His own
    Silence-Light.

296. WHEN YOU HAVE SET ASIDE YOUR IGNORANCE

When you have set aside your pride,
Then God will definitely show you
Special affection.

When you have set aside your doubt,
Then God will definitely claim you
As His very own.

When you have set aside your love of
    ignorance-night,
Then God will definitely immortalise you
By revealing your all-illumining Goal to you.

297. BE A BELIEVER

If your faith is narrow
You cannot have a naked sword
To stab the pride of ignorance.

Be a believer, a God-believer
Through your love-life,
Devotion-breath,
Surrender-heart.
God will not only lighten your task
But also enlighten your path.

298. GOD'S BIRTHDAY PRESENT

On my birthday
God came to me
And answered a question of mine:
"God, what do you do all the time?"
He said, "I do nothing but listen,
Listen to the world's deplorable fate
And ever-changeable fate
And to
Heaven's satisfaction-glory
And creation-unification story."

299. MASTERY

Mastery is a great thing!
Unless I reach the liberty-goal,
How can I acquire mastery?
Or unless I am always alive in You,
How can I acquire mastery?

300. GIVE NOTHING AWAY

Give nothing away.
Not even ignorance,
For the transformation of ignorance
Can be and is the extended perfection
Of God's Omnipresence-Reality.

301. ALL I HAVE TO MY NAME

All I have to my name
Is Your Compassion-flood.
All I have to my name
Is Your Concern-sky.
All I have to my name
Is Your Love-sun.

302. THE RUNNER IN ME

In the inner life
Hope is good
   for the beginner runner in me,
Certainty is good
   for the expert runner in me,
Triumph is good
   for the champion runner in me.

303. GOOD FRIENDS

Hope has a good friend:
Compassion human.

Certainty has a good friend:
Satisfaction divine.

304. INFINITUDE MUST BE BORN

Gratitude
Must be born
With the aspiring human man.

Infinitude
Must be born
With the life-surrendering God-man.

305. EVERYBODY BUT ME

Everybody wants to grow,
But
I want to glow.

Everybody wants to receive,
But
I want to achieve.

Everybody wants success-sound,
But
I want progress-silence.

306. THE RIGHT THING TO DO

If you are really great
Then speak humbly of humility.
This is undoubtedly the right thing to do.

If you are really good
Then speak silently of divinity.
This is unquestionably the right thing to do.

307. I HAVE KNOWN IT ALL ALONG

High imagination is nature's equal.
I have known it all along.

Devoted service is meditation's equal.
I have known it all along.

308. THE ONLY JOY IN THE WORLD

The only joy
In the outer world
Is to begin.

The only joy
In the inner world
Is to continue.

The only joy
In God's world
Is never to stop,
But to unconditionally love God
And serve His creation.

309. THREE FAULTS OF THE MIND

Three faults of the mind:
It overeats the suspicion-cake;
It humiliates its best friend, heart;
It suspects its own existence-reality-light.

310. SUCH IS HOPE

Such is hope:
It tells us what to do,
But it does not
Teach us how to do it.

Such is hope:
It tells us that God is appearing,
But alas, who appears?
Frustration-monster.

311. WHAT THEY ARE TO EACH OTHER

Purity is to the body
What clarity is to the mind.

Gratitude is to the heart
What infinitude is to the soul.

312. MY GOD IS MANY

Your God is but one God.
He is great;
I do not deny it.

My God is many.
They are not only great
but also good.

Because of their greatness,
In Heaven they dance and dance.
Because of their goodness,
On earth they cry and cry.

313. CONFLICTING PHILOSOPHIES

The body is just a thing;
Don't waste your time on it.
My philosopher-friend has taught me this.

The body is a temple in which to worship God;
Appreciate it, admire it, love it.
My Yogi-friend has taught me this.

314. A LONG-TREASURED THOUGHT

O Lord Supreme,
You are my possibility-Heaven.
You are my inevitability-manifestation.

O Lord Supreme,
In You I never have a thought.
But today I offer You a long-treasured thought:
I need You, I constantly need You,
Badly and sleeplessly.

315. HIS LIFE-COLOURS

His heart is made of gratitude gold.
His mind is made of fortitude bold.
His life is made of infinitude blue.
He lives only for the manifestation
Of God-Promise here on earth.

316. HIS GOD-LIFE

His eyes are made of the beauty of the stars.
His arms are made of the duty of the sun.
His head is made of the beauty of the moon.
His life belongs not to him
But to the God-Vision operating in humanity.
His life is divinity's progress in humanity's
   success.

317. IF

If you are not humble,
You will definitely stumble.
If you are not pure,
You can never be sure.
If you are not sincere,
You can never conquer fear.
If you believe,
Then you will not only receive
But you will also achieve
What God infinitely has
And eternally is.

318. WHAT TO DO?

What to do?
Don't you know?
Stick to one thing:
Love God.
Stick to something more:
Obey God.
Finally, one thing more:
Think that God is for you to use at every
   moment
In the march of changes
In ageless time.

319. COMPLETING THE GAME

Yesterday you believed,
Today you are obeying,
Tomorrow you will complete your game
By becoming God the Dream-Boat
   and
God the Reality-Shore.

320. ARE YOU BEGINNING TO BELIEVE?

Are you beginning to believe?
Then you have made tremendous progress.
Are you beginning to obey?
Then you have made tremendous progress.
Are you beginning to surrender?
Then you have made all the progress
That a human being in a mortal frame
Can ever achieve.

321. DO YOU LOVE GOD?

Do you love God?
Then do Him a favour.
Just reform yourself.
Then your necessity of God
Will loom large
And God's necessity of you
Will find its perfection-satisfaction
In your life's inner cry
   and
Your heart's outer smile.

322. THE COMPASSION-LIGHT FROM ABOVE

Necessity does not reform us.
It is the Compassion-light from above
That reforms us.
Reality does not fulfil us,
It is the Compassion-light,
It is the Satisfaction-concern from above
That reforms us, fulfils us
And
Glorifies us.

323. DO NOT REGRET

Regret is nothing but a waste;
Therefore, do not regret.
See the light, feel the light, become the light
Of today's dawn
And try not, cry not
To see yesterday's stars, moon and sun.
They are gone.
They should be buried in oblivion-night.

324. IF YOU LOVE TO BECOME ONE

If you like to obey,
Then you can go far.
If you love to surrender,
Then you will go very far.
If you love to become consciously,
   constantly
    and inseparably one
    with God-Light,
Then not only will you reach the farthest
But you have already reached
The farthest of all.

325. HE LIVES FOR OTHERS

He lives for others.
His confidence in God
Satisfies others,
Pleases others,
Fulfils others.

He lives for others.
He is the soul-light of God-world's Beauty's
All-illumining Height.

326. LIVE WHERE YOU ARE

Live where you are.
I shall not try to convert you.
I shall not inject fear into you.

Live where you are.
Only grow confidence indomitable within
　　yourself
So that in you can loom large
God-necessity
And
God-satisfaction Reality.

327. I AM ONE OF THOSE FEW

I cannot exactly say who loved God first,
Or who needed God first,
But this much I can say:
I am one of those few, very few
Who need God first,
Who love God first
Long before they think of themselves,
　　love themselves.

328. GOD-LOVE IS ONE THING

God-love is one thing.
If you do not stick to that very thing,
How can God love you,
How can God transform you?
Keep one thought, one will, one soul, one goal.
Then God will not only love you and need you,
But claim you immediately, for Eternity,
As His very own,
His very own.

329. DIVINITY'S DELIGHT

Sincerity
Is Eternity's delight.

Humility
Is Immortality's delight.

Purity
Is Divinity's delight.

330. ONLY TWO THINGS

Lord, I wish to learn
Only two things from You:
How I can always
Remain at Your Feet;
How I can always
Breathe in Your ever-transcending
Consciousness-Delight.

331. I LOVE THE WORLD BECAUSE

I love the world
Not because
The world loves me,
Not because
God loves me.

I love the world
Because
I know nothing else to do,
Because
I want nothing else to do.

332. LOOK AT MY GOD

I am not the only failure.
Look at my God.
He is suffering excruciating pangs.

I am not the only success.
Look at my God.
He is dancing with me His dance,
His life-immortalising Nectar-dance.

333. NOTHING WRONG

There was nothing wrong
In my trying to see God;
Therefore
I sincerely tried.

There is nothing wrong
In my crying to see God smile;
Therefore
I am devotedly crying.

334. GOD-COMPASSION HAS DEVOURED ME

Only my love of God
Is good in my life.
The rest is hopeless and useless.

But God says
Everything in my life is good,
For God-Compassion has totally devoured me,
My all.

335. THOUGHT-EXPERIMENTS

Explode a thought,
Happiness deserts you.

Explore a thought,
Surprise envelops you.

Implore a thought,
Helplessness befriends you.

336. I DO NOT KNOW

I do not know
Who God is.

I do not want to know
How ignorant humanity is.

I do not and cannot know
If an unaspiring man
Can always be pleased with God.

337. TO KNOW YOU A LITTLE BETTER

To know you a little better
Is to make significant progress
In the inner life.
To know you a little better
Is to run towards the summit
Of success-hill.

To stay more in you, less in me:
This is the only way
I can see the face of
Perfection-delight.
There is no other way,
There is no other way.

338. I SHALL NOT CRITICISE

I shall not criticise
Either man or God,
For man tries
In spite of being helpless
And
God tries
In spite of arriving uninvited.

339. YOU WILL BE HAPPY

Think beyond humanity
You will be happy.

Think within divinity.
You will be happier.

Live in humanity to manifest divinity.
You will be the happiest.

340. JUST CRY FOR TRUTH

Stings of falsehood:
Easy to remove.
Just cry for truth,
Live for truth,
Surrender to truth,
Please the truth
In its own way.

341. LET US GO INTO THE SILENCE-ROOM

O my mind,
Let us go into the silence-room.
I assure you,
You will be happy,
You will be illumined,
You will be fulfilled.

O my mind,
Let us go into the silence-room.
It is the silence-room that can give you
What you have always wanted:
Peace, peace.

342. EACH NEW DAY

Each new day
Is a gift.

Each new day
Is opportunity's revelation-sky.

Each new day
Is reality's manifestation-sun.

343. LORD, PRESERVE US

Lord, preserve us
From false peace-givers,
From false prophets,
From false Masters.
Earth-turmoil is more than enough
To buffet us.
Let us not be victims
Of false saviours.

344. THE ONLY WAY

Sometimes I must be silent,
For that is the only way
To know a little better,
To think a little wiser,
To become a little more perfect,
To claim God a little sooner.

345. IN ANOTHER DAY

I see my world
In another day,
Not in today's cry.

I see my world
In another day,
Not in tomorrow's smile.

346. JUST KEEP ME FROM LETHARGY-SIGHT

Lord,
You do not have to keep me from failure-night.
Just keep me from lethargy-sight,
   from incapacity-frustration,
   from impurity-destruction.

347. I HAVE GIVEN YOU THE RIGHT

Lord, You have granted me courage to change.
I have given You the right to transform me,
Perfect me,
Fulfil Yourself in me.
This right I have given You
With cheerfulness-light
And
Surrender-delight.

348. SUPREME LORD, SAVE ME

Supreme Lord,
Save me from all self-complacency.
Free me from all the invasions of fear.
Give me the capacity to tackle fear-night.
Lord Supreme,
To You I offer my Eternity's gratitude,
Because I am now all awake.

349. PRIDE HAS RUINED ME

My youth-enamoured pride
Has ruined me.
Unless, indeed, I dwell
With humility-breath,
Destruction-night shall embrace
My helplessness-heart.

350. THE CHILD OF YOUR FORGIVENESS

Bad am I, but yet
The child of Your Forgiveness,
The child of Your Compassion,
The child of Your Dream-boat,
The child of Your Reality-shore.

351. O GIVER OF THYSELF

O Giver of Thyself,
You have given me
More than I deserve,
Infinitely more than I deserve.
To You I have given
My aspiration-cry,
My realisation-smile,
And
My determination-perfection.

352. IF SO IS THY WILL

I am not mine own.
I know not what to say.
I move around with my beggarly heart.
I forgive myself,
My stupidity,
My existence-night
Only for Thee
To please Thee,
If so is Thy Will.

353. I HAVE CONQUERED GOD

My obedience
Has conquered God's Compassion.
My service
Has conquered God's Smile.
My love
Has conquered God's Oneness.

354. WHO HAS FREED ME?

Who has freed me
From confusion-thought?
My eternal Friend, God.

Who has made to dawn on me
Possibilities of Divinity's life?
My old Friend, God.

Who has given me
The capacity to transcend
Every day, every hour,
My existence-reality?
My God, my Beloved Supreme.

355. OF THEE, FOR THEE

My desire is before Thee,
My aspiration is in Thee,
My satisfaction is for Thee.
I am of Thy Compassion-Light,
For Thy Satisfaction-Delight.

356. IMPURITY HAS ROBBED YOUR LIFE

Impurity has robbed your life.
Go back to your aspiration-source
Slowly and steadily.

Think of God, dream of God.
He will catch your impurity-thief
Quickly and readily.

357. THEY ARE AFRAID

He is afraid of something:
The unavoidable shadow
Of his impurity-life.

She is afraid of something:
The constant absence
Of God-satisfaction
In her insecurity-heart.

358. I OCCUPIED MYSELF WITH PRAYER

I occupied myself with prayer;
Therefore
God-cries welcomed me.

I occupied myself with prayer;
Therefore
God wanted me to sit at His Feet.

I occupied myself with prayer;
Therefore
God wanted me to touch His Heart.

I occupied myself with prayer;
Therefore
God wanted me to dine with Him
In silence,
In the height
Of His Transcendental Silence-glory.

359. THE FINAL PROOF OF GOD

What is the final proof of God?
It is that you are not afraid of Him.
What is the final proof of God?
It is that you know
He claims you as His very own.
Whether you claim Him or not,
He leaves all to you
And claims you as His very own.

360. BE NOT AFRAID

Be not afraid of greatness.
Greatness cannot devour you.

Be not puzzled by earth-achievements.
They do not mark Immortality's Life.

Be not afraid of anything.
Love everything.
But grow into one thing only:
God-Delight.

361. A GIANT TREE OF HOPE

Inside you I see
Tender leaves of hope.
How I wish to see inside you
A giant tree of hope
That will weather the buffets of darkness
And the torrents of ignorance-night.

362. BE PURE!

Be pure!
Otherwise, you will see the sinking flame.

Be pure
And God will give you the keys
To open His three doors:
Realisation,
Perfection,
Satisfaction –
Realisation in life,
Perfection in the entire being,
Satisfaction both on earth
And in Heaven,
Both in God's Dream-existence
And in God's Reality-existence.

363. THE WINGS OF FRIENDSHIP

The wings of earth-friendship
Fly very fast,
Sooner than at once.
We see them
But
They fly beyond, far beyond our ken.

The wings of Heaven comradeship
Slowly,
  steadily,
  unerringly fly
And
We can follow them easily
To the shores of Infinity's
Peace,
Light
  and
Delight.

364. SHORT ROADS

The road that leads
From fear to doubt
Is very short.

The road that leads
From doubt to destruction
Is very short.

The road that leads
From sincerity to aspiration
Is very short.

The road that leads
From faith to Immortality
Is very short.

365. HOPE ITSELF IS HAPPINESS

Hope itself is happiness.
It needs no outer happiness
To add to its joy.

Love itself is satisfaction.
It needs no outer satisfaction
To add to its reality-strength.

366. DO ME A FAVOUR, LORD

O Lord Supreme,
Do me a favour.
Can You be from now on
My only magnet,
To save me,
To pull me towards You?
I have set aside everything
That I once upon a time claimed as my own:
Fear,
Doubt,
Bondage,
Darkness
And ignorance.
Now I want only to be
Claimed by You,
By Your Compassion-Delight alone.

367. REVEAL YOUR HUMILITY-LIFE

O voice of my weeping night,
Be not silent.
Reveal, express your humility-life!
Oneness-delight will rule your life
When you have reached
The goal of your destination-dance.

368. HELPLESS IS MY INDEPENDENCE

Helpless is my independence, Lord.
Do You know why, Lord?
Because Your Smile is not there
In my independence.
Your Concern is not there
In my independence.
What I have is only
My authority human
And
My autocracy animal.

369. HIS GREATNESS AND HIS GOODNESS

His greatness has not made him good.
On the contrary,
His greatness has ruined him.

His goodness has not only made him great
But has also made him
Eternity's indispensable necessity.

370. SIDE BY SIDE WITH ME

Lord Supreme,
My doubting mind melts
Only when You smile through my tears
And stay with me,
Play with me,
Sing with me,
And
Accomplish Your Manifestation-Light
Side by side with me.

371. LIFE'S OCCUPATIONS

The body sinks,
The vital dies,
The mind questions,
The heart suffers,
The soul smiles.

372. YOU ARE THE ONE WHO IS ALL TO ME

I saw You either yesterday
Or centuries earlier.
You are the One who is all to me.
I remain just the same,
But every hour,
Every minute,
Every second,
I see You with an ever-increasing
Sea of Compassion-light
And
Benediction-height.

373. TWO PRIZES FROM GOD

On his death day
He won two prizes from God:
Earth's satisfaction in his action
And
Heaven's unprecedented pride in his action.

374. HUMAN BELIEF AND DIVINE BELIEF

Human belief is wounded.
It needs a bandage.

Divine belief is always perfect.
It dances with the heart's rising sun
And sings with the mind's setting sun.

375. WHO IS YOUR PARTNER?

Is death your partner?
Then your life is a faded thought.

Is life your partner?
Then your life is every day a Christmas gift,
A Christ-gift.

376. HIS HOPE

His hope has grown old,
But it has offered no life-transforming,
Life-nourishing fruits.
His hope has given him
A Heavenward prayer.
In that prayer he creates
His garden of Love-Light.

377. NO RIVALRY

Between God and man
There is no rivalry.
Man needs God to realise
What he eternally is.
God needs man to see
What he can eventually become.

378. TIME SERVES US

Time serves us,
Space serves us,
God loves us,
Hope feeds us,
Truth directs us,
Gratitude teaches us.

379. SEE ME IN MY HEART'S GLORY

Don't see me with a questioning mind.
Don't see me with a strangling thought.
My Heaven is already falling.
If you want to see me,
See me in my heart's morning glory.

380. A NECESSITY PARAMOUNT

The body calls it death,
The soul calls it an experience,
God calls it a necessity paramount
At this present state
Of life's evolving wheel.

381. REMAIN IN THE LOVING AND SERVING HEART

The preparation for your life's new lease
Gives you joy.
This time keep away from intellect-snare.
Remain only in the loving heart
Of God's faith in you.

382. YOU ARE BOUND TO SUCCEED

If you want to satisfy ambition,
You will fail.
If you want to satisfy your ideal,
You will fail.
If you want to satisfy God-necessity
In yourself,
In others
And in the heart of the world,
You will certainly succeed;
You are bound to succeed.

383. RESPONSIBILITY WEIGHS HIM DOWN

Earth-responsibility weighs him down.
Heaven-responsibility weighs him down.
God-responsibility weighs him down.
Yet he smiles at God,
Cries with earth
And
Sinks for Heaven.

384. TO DANCE WITH SATISFACTION-PERFECTION

My faith in You
Is my pride in You.

To have pride in You
Is to long for You.

To long for You
Is to dance
With satisfaction-perfection.

385. MEDITATION

Meditation upon the unknown Thought
He thought was real meditation.
No, meditation is not and cannot be
On any thought.
Meditation is a conscious withdrawal
From the thought-world.
Meditation is the place
Where Reality, Divinity and Immortality
Can each claim their own
Perennial existence-light.

386. NOW IS THE TIME

Now is the time to flee
From fruitless desire.

Now is the time to learn
That there is nothing certain on earth.

Now is the time to realise
That I need no other thing except
   God-Compassion;
I need no other human being
But God, my eternal Father.

387. I OFFER MY EXISTENCE TO YOU

My sad thoughts I offer to You,
My glad thoughts I offer to You,
My desire-life I offer to You,
My aspiration-life I offer to You.
I offer to You my divine existence,
Which is faith supreme,
And my human existence,
Which is Himalayan pride.

388. PARDON MY INGRATITUDE

Lord Supreme, pardon my ingratitude.
Faithlessness gave birth to my ingratitude.
Today Your Feet I embrace
With my heart's faithfulness-cry.
Lo, I am changed!
Your Compassion-Eye has changed me
Into gratitude-heart.

389. THE OBJECT

The object of all human thought:
Success-glory.

The object of all divine Will:
Perfection-progress.

390. THIS I KNOW FOR SURE

Your hope for me
Shall sustain me.
This I know for sure.

You will guide me
On my way to God.
This I know for sure.

My life has now become
A trial fatal.
My life's only true need
Is Your Love,
Your Love alone.
This I know for sure.

391. I UNBURDEN MYSELF IN GOD

I unburden myself
In God;
Therefore
I am no longer
Soulless, lifeless.
Happiness I desired
By pleasing God
With purity's breath;
Therefore
Happiness-heart,
Happiness-soul
Once and for all
I have gained.

392. IN SUPREME GRATITUDE

Lord,
I wish to shine
In supreme gratitude;
Therefore
I am awake,
I am walking,
I am running,
Towards the golden Destination-dance.

Lord, many a time
You have forgiven me.
Just forgive me this one more time.
With my ever-undying gratitude
I shall leave You alone in peace,
For good.

393. THY WILL IS MY PEACE

Lord,
Today at long last
I have lost
The fear of failure;
Therefore
I have become Thy Will.
Thy Will alone is my peace,
My Eternity's peace,
My Immortality's peace,
My Reality's peace.

394. IN SWEET DREAMS I SLEEP

In sweet dreams
I sleep.
In bitter realities
I strive to live.

In God-dreams
I am enlightened.
In man-realities
I am frightened.

395. YET MY CHILDREN LOVE ME

How little do I serve,
Yet my children love me dearly.
How little do I love,
Yet my children need me constantly.
Their humility-life and oneness-necessity
Feed me daily and still keep me alive.

396. WHAT IS EARTH-BEAUTY?

What is earth-beauty?
Earth-beauty is something momentary.
It lives in the mind,
With the mind,
For the mind.

397. UNFORESEEN MISFORTUNES

Three unforeseen misfortunes:
Ignorance loves me,
Darkness threatens me,
Self-doubt devours me.

398. HE IS CERTAIN

He is certain
Of his uncertainty.

He is certain
Of the victory of his doubt-life.

He is certain
Of his incapacity-train.

He is certain
Of his bondage-chain.

399. FEVER OF THE WORLD

Fever of the world:
Fear.

Headache of the world:
Worry.

Cancer of the world:
Doubt.

Death of the world:
Ingratitude.

400. THE WORLD IS CHANGING

The animal world is changing,
Changing for the better.
It feels that human beings
Not only want it but need it.

The human world is changing,
Changing for the better.
It has come to know that divine beings
Will definitely manifest themselves in and
 through it.

401. DEATH VISITED HIM TWICE

Death visited him twice:
Once when he said,
"I am ignorant";
Once when he said,
"God does not love me."

402. THREE EYES OF GOD

Three Eyes of God:
Each one does something special.

He uses
The Eye that is inside His Head
To see if I have done
Anything wrong.

He uses
The Eye that is inside His Heart
To see if I have done
Everything perfectly.

He uses
The Eye that is at His Feet
To teach me how to do
Everything in perfect perfection.

403. LESSONS FROM GOD

Yesterday
God taught me
How to smile soulfully.

Today
God is teaching me
How to cry ceaselessly.

Tomorrow
God will teach me
How to surrender consciously,
Cheerfully,
Constantly
And unconditionally.

404. THOUGHT-PATTERNS

You think very silently;
Therefore
Nobody likes you.

He thinks very loudly;
Therefore
Nobody likes him.

I think very differently;
Therefore
Nobody loves me.

405. DOUBT WILL UNDOUBTEDLY FAIL

The ancient doubt
Has come.
The brave demand
Its God-identity.
Doubt will undoubtedly fail
To show its world-passport.
The brave start smiling
And continue smiling
Until the Goal of goals,
God-satisfaction,
Is won.

406. LIVE WITH MUSIC

Live with God-music.
It will make you immortal.

Live with man-music.
It will make you cry and sigh.

Live with animal-music.
It will strangle you and devour you.

407. SHARED PATIENCE

The patience that we share
With the stone-consciousness
Of earthly beings
Wins God's blessingful Vision
And
God's fruitful Reality.

408. A SEEKER

A seeker is he
Who is full of tomorrow's world.

A seeker is he
Who believes in tomorrow's smile,
And not in today's cry.

409. THE MEDITATION OF THE EARTH

The meditation of the secret earth
Is all for its personal realisation.

The meditation of the sacred earth
Is all for God-manifestation,
For God-satisfaction.

410. HIS ACTION-LIFE

His body breathes like a prayer.
His heart smiles like a flower.
His soul dances at God's Hour.
His vital and mind fight against ignorance-sea
To worship God-Tower.

411. THE DANCER

Heart-peace retires,
Body-suffering appears.
Peace revives,
Suffering is abolished.
Lo, who is dancing
Eternity's life-feeding,
Life-immortalising Dance?
It is God.

412. THE MOTHER OF TIME

Time itself has fallen asleep
With you.
Who will wake you up?
Nobody knows.
No, not even the Mother of Time:
Truth, Reality's satisfaction-dawn.

413. SUCCESS IS YOURS

I pray with every breath
To serve God in man
And
To love man in God.

Have I succeeded?
Not yet!
Will I ever succeed?
I am uncertain.

But God says,
"Son, success is yours.
Only wait for My choice Hour."

414. NO POWER OVER HIM

Earth-time has no power over him.
He is timeless.
World-temptation has no power over him.
He is his own Heaven perfection-satisfaction.

415. TO ESCAPE THE FLAME OF GOD-UNION

O weak seeker,
To escape the flame of God-union
Is to suffer the furnace
Of beginningless and
Endless death.

416. TRY, SMILE AND CRY

To try
Is to love God.
To smile
Is to fulfil God.
To cry
Is to serve God.

417. LORD, GIVE ME THE STRENGTH

Lord,
Give me the human strength
To love the animal
In Your creation vast.

Lord,
Give me the divine strength
To illumine the human
In Your creation vast.

Lord,
Give me the supreme strength
To immortalise the divine
In Your creation vast.

418. THEY NEED EACH OTHER

His will is as pure as snow;
Therefore
God needs him.

God's Compassion-Light is unconditional;
Therefore
He needs God and God alone.

419. THE GREATNESS OF THE SOUL

The greatness of the soul
Tells me:
"Do not leave!
Just stay in my boat.
I shall do everything for you."

420. THE LONELINESS OF THE BODY

The loneliness of the body
Tells me:
"Unless you love me,
I shall leave you.
Unless you admire me
I shall leave you.
Unless you put the soul and me
On the same footing,
I shall leave you."

421. HIS HEART IS MADE OF STARS

His heart is made of stars;
Therefore
He is beautiful.
His life is made of suns;
Therefore
He is fruitful.

422. DON'T BOAST!

The dust of time
Will smash your pride.
Don't boast!

The sneer of time
Will devour your glory's peak!
Don't boast!

423. YET HE LOVES HIS INNER LIFE

The noise of the inner vital-gramophone
Is killing him,
Yet he loves his inner life,
For he feels that
The perfection of that life
Is the only thing
That can and will satisfy him.

424. THE BEAUTY OF GOD WILL LOVE YOU

Far from the storm of vital life
If you live,
The Beauty of God,
The Divinity of God
Will love you,
Treasure you
And
Immortalise you.

425. I HAVE PLEASED GOD MAGNIFICENTLY

To scale Heaven-heights
With my heart's spontaneous smile
I finally tried
And
Easily succeeded.
Lo, God is telling me
I have pleased Him
Magnificently,
At long last.

426. O HEAVENLY BODIES

O twinkling stars,
Do take me home!
I am all ready.

O sweet moon,
Where is my Eternal Father?
I am dying to see Him.

O brave sun,
Can you fight for me?
I must conquer ignorance-night
With your unparalleled might.

427. I LIKE, I LOVE, I ENJOY

The wheel of imagination
I like.

The skill of dedication
I love.

The thrill of self-giving
I enjoy.

428. THE CULPRITS

A voice of base passion
And
A mind of God-denial
Are richly responsible
For his close embrace
With frustration-destruction.

429. THREE KEYS

Lord,
You have given me three keys.
One key is to open up
Your Eternity-door.
One key to open up
My security-door.
One key to open up
Our mutual satisfaction-door.

430. OUR JOINT DESIRE

To become a poet
Was my desire.

To make me an artist
Is God's Desire.

To make me a supreme instrument
Will be God's and my joint desire.

431. NOTHING IS CERTAIN

Nothing is certain here on earth
Or there in Heaven.
Here we try to live in faith.
Sometimes we succeed,
Sometimes we fail.
There we try to live in peace.
Sometimes we succeed,
Sometimes we do not.

432. HIS LIFE WAS SICK WITH DESIRE

His life was sick with desire.
He knew no other thing but desire.
But
There came a time
When even his desire-thoughts left him.
Then he sang the song of separation.
But
In separation he still found no peace.
He found peace
Only in the heart of aspiration-cry-tree.

433. THE SAME OLD THOUGHTS

The same old thoughts:
God does not love me,
God does not want me,
I am left all alone.
I was nothing,
I am nothing,
I shall be nothing.
These are the ideas that make my life miserable
And throw me into the very jaws of
   destruction-tiger.

O Forgiver of all my shortcomings,
Forgive me.
A new hope is being born in my heart.
I shall cry from today on
To grow into Perfection's beauty-delight.

434. I OFFER MY CAPACITY

O Lord, purify my heart,
Vivify my life.
I wish cheerfulness to preside over my existence.
Father, in Your Name
I offer my capacity
To the life of earth-beauty.

435. WHAT DOES IT MATTER?

What does it matter
If God loves me or not?
What does it matter
If God cares for me or not?
Do I love God?
If I answer this question in the affirmative,
Then there can be no reason
Why God will not love me
Or will not care for me.
God always does infinitely more for us
Than we do for Him.
He does according to His Necessity's capacity.
We do according to our capacity's necessity.

436. HE WHO UNDERSTANDS IS THE WINNER

Activity wants no rest.
Life demands victory and not defeat.
He who understands, to me, is the winner
And
He who does not understand is the loser.
Let us understand what we need:
God-compassion,
And understand what we do not need:
Our intellect-pride.

437. WHAT HE DOES AND WHAT HE SAYS

What he does
Only God and he know.
What he says
He knows and his friends know,
Both earth and Heaven know.

His action bears fruit
Inside the Heart of God.
His speech bears fruit
Inside the heart of aspiring and glowing
 humanity.

438. AN OLD DISEASE

Doubt is an old disease.
Faith is an old medicine.
Compassion is an old doctor.
Concern is an old nurse.

439. REALLY BAD, REALLY GOOD

Nothing will surprise me.
Everything is possible here on earth.
But what is really bad
And what is really good?
To escape from reality-life
Is really bad.
To fight against ignorance
And to establish wisdom-light
Is really good.

440. WHERE IS GRATITUDE?

Where is gratitude?
Inside the heart of man?
No!
Inside the mind of man?
No!
Inside the entire body of man?
No!
Where is it?
It is inside the soulful tears
Of the seeker's climbing eyes.

441. YOU HAVE LOST YOUR PEACE

You were once so secure.
What is wrong with you?
I am sure you have lost your mental peace;
Therefore
You are behaving
Like a street-beggar.

442. TOO STRONG TO SURRENDER

I am too old to be taught.
I am too young to be caught.
I am too weak to fight.
I am too strong to surrender.

443. HIS SMILE

His smile
Is the fragrance of the soul.
His smile
Is the lustre of the Beyond.
His smile
Is man's trust in God
And
God's trust in man.

444. HE WHO TRUSTS HIS HEART

He who trusts his mind is a fool.
Indeed, he has to pay the penalty for his stupidity.
He who trusts his heart
Is not only a wise man
But *the* wise man,
For his heart always,
Like a magnet,
Pulls Wisdom-Light
From the Delight-Source of the soul.

445. DO NOT BETRAY ME, LORD

Do not betray me, Lord,
Do not kill me, Lord,
For I am Yours.
Your Smile is my food.
Your Tears are my earth-realisation's
Ultimate height.

446. THE TEMPLE OF SILENCE

The Temple of Silence
Can tell me
How earth-perfection can come into existence,
Or it can tell me
How destruction-night can invite me
And devour me.

447. THE ESSENCE OF DIVINITY

The opportunity to do more
Is the affirmation of service-reality.
The essence of divinity
Is a glimpse of Eternity.

448. THE REDEMPTION OF IGNORANCE

How to learn?
Pursue the truth,
Will to believe,
Spread the inner radiance.
Then alone
The redemption of ignorance
Can take place.

449. GOD GAVE ME THE OPPORTUNITY

God gave me the opportunity
To do infinitely more
Than what I do now.
But my lethargy-life permits me not
To offer more dedication-service
To the heart of man's oneness-height.

450. THE PRISONER

He is the prisoner
Of his own experience.
He is the prisoner
Of his own realisation.
He is the prisoner
Of what he says and does.
He knows the secret ways
Of the universe.
Nothing,
Nothing gives him joy.
He is crying to restore the forgotten paradise.

451. EVERYTHING KILLS HIM

Worry kills him,
Anxiety kills him
Fear kills him,
Doubt kills him,
Everything kills him.
But
He can be saved
Not only from one thing
But from everything,
Provided he has the willingness
To follow the dictates
Of the inner Source.

452. FASTEST HE RUNS

His inner life
Is the loveliness of perfection-deeds.
His outer life
Is the flow of beauty's light
And duty's glow.
He never drags the broken mind;
Therefore
Fast, faster, fastest he runs
Towards his destination-smile.

453. GOD IS BEYOND COMPREHENSION

If you are incapable of understanding
God's operation in and through you,
Do not feel sad,
For God is beyond comprehension.
But if you can love Him
And love Him,
Then your life will celebrate
The blossom of your oneness-power
With God.

454. HE LOOKS BEAUTIFUL

He looks beautiful
In eternal Silence.
He looks soulful
In eternal Sound.
He looks fruitful
In eternal surrender
To God-Reality,
To God-Divinity.

455. HIS IS THE CHOICE

His is the vital that likes to live
In the abyss of confusion.
His innate weakness disturbs his soul
   immensely.

His is the heart of humiliation.
Alone he goes,
Alone, blessedly.

His is the enlightening opinion,
His is the enlightened conviction,
His is the choice that moves his heart.
His only happiness is his heart's inner nuclear
   will.

456. I AM TEACHING GOD, TOO

My self-giving
Is my God-becoming.
This is what God
Has so kindly taught me.
I am teaching God something too:
Patience.

457. REALITY IS NEAR, REALITY IS FAR

Reality is near,
Reality is far.
When I say God and I
Need each other,
Reality is near
And
I can touch it.
When I say I only need God
Or God only needs me,
Then reality is not only far,
But also hopelessly invisible.

458. HIS IS THE SOUL

His is the Eye
That watches the world
With Compassion.

His is the Heart
That loves the world
With benediction.

His is the Soul
That fulfils the world
With salvation's realisation.

459. HE IS HIS OWN PERPETUAL HOPE

He is
His own perpetual hope;
Therefore
God loves him.

He is
His own perpetual disappointment;
Therefore
God instructs him.

460. THE REALISATION IN MY LIFE

The realisation that is yet to become
True in my life
Shall far surpass
Not only my expectation-light
But also
My imagination-flight.

461. MY DESIRE-HEART

My desire-heart is not alone.
It has discovered its friends:
The furrows of frustration-poverty
And
Destruction-futility.

462. NO WALLS CAN PROTECT ME

What walls can protect me?
No walls.

What life can elevate me?
No life.

What success can immortalise me?
No success.

463. HE IS PLEASED WITH EVERYTHING

He was
Pleased with nothing;
Therefore
God was not pleased with him.

He is now
Pleased with everything;
Therefore
God has given him two things:
Satisfaction-throne,
Perfection-crown.

464. I DARE, I HOPE

I dare to hope;
Therefore
The dying man in me smiles.

I hope to dare;
Therefore
The challenging man in me smiles.

465. SAD MUSIC, GLAD MUSIC

The sad music of humanity:
Sigh-cry-die.

The glad music of divinity:
Smile-love-serve.

466. NOW HE IS INSEPARABLY ONE

Man's most desired light
Is in his heart's inner cry.
There his wisdom rules;
His eyes have the healing touch.
His is the life that was
Once-upon-a-time
A weak human cry.
But now he is inseparably one
With endless height
And
With endless delight.

467. O DAWN OF LIFE

O dawn of life,
You I need
To run and fly
Into the unknown.

O life of dawn,
Beautiful you are,
Soulful you are,
Fruitful you are,
God's Eternity-Dream you are.

468. WHERE IS HOPE?

Where is hope?
Hope is not in outer
Liberty-school.
Hope is not in outer
Perfection-choice.
Hope is in inner
Self-giving,
Which is eventually known as
God-becoming.

469. HIS LOVE FED ME

His love fed me,
His concern blessed me,
His oneness-sincerity
Immortalised me,
My all.

470. GOD ALONE KNOWS

God alone knows
Who I am,
What kind of love I have
For Him,
How strong is my will of steel
For Him,
How soon my salvation-light
Shall dawn.

471. I CAME IN VAIN

I have a helpless heart,
Two hopeless hands
And two sightless eyes.
I came to enjoy
My earthbound journey.
But
In vain I spent my journey's
Birth and death.

472. TOUCH HIM

Touch him with Compassion-power;
Even then he offers no response.
Touch him with restriction-power;
Even then he pays no heed.
Touch him with determination-power;
Still he pays no attention.
But
Touch him with oneness-realisation-light,
And he comes and sits at your feet.

473. I CAN GO BACK TO THE SOURCE

Everything has roots.
My root is in the God-Source.
I can go back to that Source
When everything drops away
And
When I drop away from desire-night
And from indifference-sky.

474. YOUR LOVE-SERVICE IS PERFECT

Your love-service is perfect;
Your service-love is perfect.
You have opened the gates
Of a new life.
There was a time when you were
The clumsiness of feebleness.
But now you are
The delight of beauty's height
And of God-necessity's smile.

475. YOU WILL BE HAPPY

Open the gates of a new life.
You will be happy.
Close the gates of your old life.
You will be happy.
Offer your service-light to God in man.
You will be happy.
Offer your satisfaction-promise to man in God.
You will be happy.

476. THE FOLLY OF MAN

The folly of man!
He desires revelation before realisation.
He is afraid to climb high.
His concentration on truth
Threatens him and frightens him.
Alas, he is always assailed
By destructive memories.
Oblivion-life:
This is what he feels he needs
To perfect his life in God's Dream.

477. HE HAS A PURE HEART

He has a pure heart.
In spite of having human insufficiencies,
He desires the union
Of spirit's height
And
Wisdom's vision-light.

478. MAKE YOUR OWN CHOICE

If you are dear to God's Voice
You have to make your own choice.
You have to be the ruler
Of your life
Or
You have to be the fulfiller
Of your desire-train.

479. I SAT ON SILENCE-CHAIR

I sat on silence-chair.
My doubt-mind was frightened to death;
Therefore
It did not sit.
My faith-heart sat with me
And listened to Reality's Voice
And
Divinity's Song.

480. YOUR FAME SHALL GROW

Your fame shall grow
If your inner flame glows.
O sincerity-wisdom,
Your inner cry
Is your outer
Success-glory
And
Progress-story.

481. ONLY SPIRITUALITY CAN GIVE HIM REST

Only equality
Can give his heart rest.
Only equanimity
Can give his mind rest.
Only divinity
Can give his soul rest.
Only spirituality
Can give his life rest.

482. I SHALL GIVE YOU EVERYTHING

I shall give you a chance
If you will take a chance.
I shall give you a new life
If you will take a new life.
I shall give you everything you need,
But it is you who have to take it from me.
In your cheerful acceptance-light
Is your life's perfection-manifestation.

483. INSUFFICIENCY HUMAN AND SUFFICIENCY DIVINE

When he lives in the body
Insufficiency human is his name.
When he lives in the soul
Sufficiency divine is his name.

484. HE LIVES IN HIS FEARS AND DOUBTS

In his world there is no plan.
In his life there is no idea.
In his heart there is no idea.
He lives in his baseless fears
And
In his graceless doubts.

485. GOD WILL APPEAR

When his majesty is melted
God will appear before him.
When his insecurity is well-exposed
God will appear before him.

486. HIS IS THE DESTINY GRANDIOSE

He lives in a world without a plan.
His is the destiny grandiose.
From the cradle unto the grave
He sings and smiles and dances.
His beginning is beautiful,
His ending is soulful and fruitful.

487. CHILDREN

Earth
Is a child of regress.

Heaven
Is a child of progress.

I
Am a child of God's evolving process.

488. HOW FAR?

My unassisted heart,
How far can you go?
I feel really sorry for you.

My powerful soul,
How far will you go?
I hope I can struggle and follow you.

489. OUR LIVES

Yours is a life
Of illumining flames.

His is a life
Of struggling aims.

Mine is a life
Of God's unconditional
Perfection-Grace.

490. THE DIFFERENCE

The difference between
A completed man
And
A complete man is this:
A completed man
Is the product of his aspiration-light.
A complete man
Is the result of God's
Perfection-Realisation-Delight.

491. DON'T MIX WITH HIM!

Don't mix with him!
He enjoys spiritual fuss.

Don't mix with him!
He indulges in spiritual jugglery.

Don't mix with him!
He shamelessly takes pride
In belittling all Masters
Except his own.

492. O MY SOUL, O MY BODY

O my soul,
Let me wing with you
On your Heaven-bound flight.

O my body,
Let me crawl with you, stumble with you
On your journey towards uncertainty's smile.

493. I REALLY FEEL SORRY FOR HIM

I really feel sorry for him.
Yesterday
He trembled before despair.
Today
He trembles before doubt.
Tomorrow
He will tremble before hope.

494. A PERFECT HOUSE OF LIGHT

His was
A perfect house of light
When he loved God.

His is now
A perfect house of night.
Why?
Because he loves and will love
Only himself,
Ceaselessly, if not shamelessly.

495. I KNOW NOT WHY

My life is a faded leaf,
Yet my Lord encourages me to live;
I know not why.

My life is a failing heart,
Yet my Lord inspires me to live;
I know not why.

My life is a destruction-sigh,
Yet my Lord commands me to live;
I know not why.

496. COME TO THE FORE

O my heart-bliss,
Come to the fore!
I need you.

O my mind-peace,
Come to the fore!
I need you.

O my life's dedication-oneness,
Come to the fore!
I need you.

497. IN THE SEA OF GOD-ECSTASY

Empty pleading hands
I offered to God
Just yesterday.

Today my heart of joy
Is full to the brim;
My surrender divine
Is swimming in the sea of God-ecstasy.

498. MY LOVE-SEED

I have sown my love-seed
In the aspiration-heart of earth.
I am sure
It will soon germinate
And grow into a huge tree
And it will offer me
Immortality's satisfaction-seed.

499. MAN'S LIFE

Slothful uncertainty:
That is man's life.

Wild impurity:
That is man's mind.

Perfect divinity:
That is man's ultimate Goal.

500. THE HEIGHTS OF CALM SURRENDER

The heights of calm surrender
I shall scale.

The depths of calm confidence
I shall plumb.

The length of calm assurance
I shall reach.

501. MY LAST RESORT

Lord,
Let me lean upon Thy Will.
This is my absolutely
Last resort.
Otherwise, life's frustration-dragon
Will devour me.

502. HE FOLLOWED FALSE LIGHTS

He followed false lights.
Now he is crying.
But never mind,
Nothing is too late.
From now on
He will follow only genuine light.
God and he will claim each other
For good.

503. THE PATIENCE OF MY LIFE'S PEAKS

The patience of my life's peaks
I love.

The forgiveness of my life's sea
I extol.

The beauty of my life's oneness-sun
I adore.

504. I DO NOT APPROVE

I do not approve of
The white comfort of the stars.

I do not approve of
The self-torturing life of unlit human beings.

505. THE DARKNESS OF HIS DOUBT

The darkness of his doubt
Frightened his mind.

The blackness of his fear
Threatened his vital.

The blindness of his insecurity
Killed his body.

506. WHO WILL UNTIE THE KNOTS?

The knots of my heart
Who will untie,
If not my forgiving soul?

The knots of my mind
Who will untie,
If not my loving heart?

The knots of my body
Who will untie,
If not my striving vital?

507. I WAS OF THREE MINDS

I was of three minds:
To love God and see God,
To love humanity and transform humanity,
Or to claim God to fulfil my own
Selfish purpose.

508. HE HAS FORGOTTEN

His are the eyes
That have forgotten to sleep.

His is the heart
That has forgotten to ignore.

His is the life
That has forgotten to negate.

509. THE DIAMOND HOPE OF THE AGES

The diamond hope for which the ages groaned
Has now opened its eye
In him
To save humanity,
To manifest divinity,
To fulfil the Absolute Supreme.

510. PROMISES

The sky promised me
It would make me high.

The ocean promised me
It would make me vast.

God promised me
He would make me
His most perfect instrument.

How I wish they all would keep
Their promises!

511. FAITH-LIFE HERE

Faith-life
Here,
Where human efforts end.

Surrender-life
Here,
Where perfection-life begins
Forever to live.

512. HEAVEN-PEACE ENVELOPS ME

Heaven-peace envelops me
When I meditate
On God's Silence-Vision.

Earth-joy envelops me
When I dedicate myself
To God's all-illumining Sound-Reality.

513. BY FAR THE GREATEST

Who shuns his earth-desires
Is great.

Who shuns his Heaven-possessions
Is greater.

Who accepts life,
Transforms life
And
Fulfils God
Is by far the greatest.

514. HE WILL UNMISTAKABLY SUCCEED

He has wasted his whole life
In a long despair.
Yet there is God-Love
For him
In abundant measure;
Therefore
He will unmistakably succeed.

515. EARTH, RUN!

Earth, sleep
If that is what you want.

Earth, run!
This is the only thing
That can enlighten you
And immortalise you
And satisfy God.

516. WRITE EARTH'S STORY

God, You have given me
A new lease on life.
Please tell me
What I shall do with it.

"Son, write earth's doleful story,
Heaven's soulful story,
And
My fruitful story."

517. TRIUMPHANT

Triumphant in silence
I wanted to be.

Triumphant in sound
I want to be.

Triumphant in God's Satisfaction
I shall want to be.

518. TO A SOUNDLESS SHORE

If you live
In Eternity's passion-chain,
How can you breathe in
Purity's compassion-flood?
Only if you do that
Will you proceed
To a soundless shore.

519. YOU ARE MY HOME

O Faith,
You are the home of my love.

O Courage,
You are the home of my success.

O Certainty,
You are the home of my progress.

O God,
You are the Home of my dream-fulfilling
  Reality.

520. OUR WHOLE EXISTENCE

Love
Is our whole being.

Devotion
Is our whole truth.

Surrender
Is our whole perfection.

Oneness
Is our whole realisation.

521. I IMMEDIATELY SAW

I looked daily for God,
But I saw many.
I looked for many,
But I saw only God.
I looked for many in God,
But I had to wait.
I looked for one in many,
And I immediately saw.

522. WHO REMEMBERS MY PROMISE?

Who remembers my promise to God?
My fate.

Who remembers my promise to mankind?
My sincerity.

Who remembers my promise to Heaven?
My conscience.

Who remembers my promise to myself?
My sincere sense of perfection.

523. IN YOU

In you I feel
Divinity's heart.
In you the world achieves
God-Reality's Perfection-Height.

524. PERFECTION-HEART

Wisdom-heart
A calm heart leaves.

Sacrifice-heart
A loving heart leaves.

Perfection-heart
A surrendered heart leaves.

525. MY BIRTHDAY SONG

My birthday song:
I plan to soar,
I plan to roar.
The bird in me
Will teach me how to soar.
The lion in me
Will teach me how to roar.
I plan to love,
Below, above.
The lover in me will teach me
How to love
Within,
Without,
Below,
Above.

526. NO WORD ABOUT YOUR REALISATION-LIGHT

God has not said a word
About your realisation-light.
He has only said
Your aspiration is good,
Your aspiration is great;
Your dedication is good,
Your dedication is great;
Your love of God is sublime,
Your prayer to God is sublime;
But He has never said a word
About your realisation-light.

527. WE DO NOT NEED YOUR HELP

God and I do not need your help.
You do not have to
Interpret God.
God is His own perfect interpreter.
You do not have to
Love me.
I am my own matchless lover.

528. DELIGHT'S ONENESS-WING

To doubt is to be disloyal.
To believe is to cover
The length and breadth of the world
With delight's oneness-wing.

529. CRY WITHIN!

Cry within!
Your heart will widen
Towards the perfection-whole.
I tell this from my own
Experience-light
And
Realisation-height.

530. WITHOUT MY LOVE

I feel God in my glowing dreams.
God sees me in my crying realities.

Without God's Love
I have nothing to live for.

Without my love
God does not want to continue
His cosmic Duty's cosmic Game.

531. HE WANTS TO KEEP GOD FOR HIMSELF

These are his own thoughts:
He wants to invite God
To his home;
He wants to keep God for himself only;
He wants to spend all his time
With God and God alone.
He will not let anybody see God's Face
Or hear about God's arrival.
He wants God only for his own
Satisfaction-necessity.

532. I AM DOING IT FOR GOD

I flung my soul into the sky.
God saw it.
He enjoyed my courage.

He now asks me
To throw my soul
Into the fathomless abyss.

Lo, I am doing it,
His Eyes to entertain,
His Heart to feed.

533. CHAMPIONS OF GOOD THOUGHTS

Love:
Discoverer of good thoughts.

Oneness:
Fulfiller of good thoughts.

Satisfaction:
Perfector of good thoughts.

534. MY EARTH-HOURS

My earth-hours are thronged with fate.
I am at the mercy of ignorance-night.
I am caught by bondage-might.
I am tortured by imperfection-sight.

535. I DO NOT ARGUE WITH GOD

Why do I not argue with God?
I do not argue with God
Not because He is great,
Not because He is good,
But because God and argument
Do not rhyme.
God transcends the argument-barrier.
For Him is the infinite, ever-transcending
Wisdom-Light.

536. GOD NEEDS YOU

Be good!
God needs you.
He needs your heart
Desperately.
He needs your life
Constantly.

537. HIS SOUL, HIS LIFE, HIS HEART

His soul
Is a present reality.

His life
Is an ancient divinity.

His heart
Is a fulfilled Immortality.

538. GOD NEEDS US

Although
Your mind is forgetful,
God needs you.

Although
His body is slothful,
God needs him.

Although
My vital is awful,
God needs me.

539. BE CAREFUL!

Be careful!
World-temptation
Will play the role
Of a hungry wolf.

Be careful!
Don't forget to expedite
Your life's illumination-journey
With your heart's mounting cry.

540. BE SILENT!

Be silent!
Your silence is your
Real progress.

Be silent!
Your silence is God's
Highest Satisfaction-Pride.

541. BE SINCERE

Be sincere.
Your sincerity feeds
The world-hunger.

Be sincere.
You can either build or break
The golden palace
Of humanity's hope-world.

542. BE PURE

Be pure.
The world needs your life of purity.
It largely depends on your love.

Be pure.
Don't disappoint
The poor helpless world.

543. WHEN HE DESCENDED

When he descended out of the morning sky
He was happy.
Beauty's Light garlanded him.
His desire itself was perfected
By divinity's touch.
He discovered that his true love of Truth
Was the shortest way to find
God the Eternal Reality.

544. THE ONLY PLACE TO BE HAPPY

This world of ours is too much.
Heaven is also too much.
Where to go?
No place in God's entire creation.
The only place to be happy
Is in the sweet dream-world,
Not in the hard reality-world.

545. AN OPEN MIND, AN OPEN HEART

You have an open mind.
Your greatness
Pleases me immediately;
Therefore
I am grateful.

You have an open heart.
Your goodness
Pleases me ceaselessly;
Therefore
I am grateful.

546. WHOM TO FEAR

Don't be afraid of human greatness.
Don't be afraid of divine goodness.
Be afraid only of the fear-thief
And the doubt-robber
And the unwilling, stubborn reluctance-life,
Reluctant to accept God-Light.

547. OUR UNITED STRENGTH

United we are
In your heart-light.

United we shall remain
In your life-sacrifice.

Our united strength
Is our perfection-voice
And
God's Satisfaction-Choice.

548. LET GOD GUIDE YOU

Let God-Compassion
Guide your plans.
This is the only way
For you to succeed.

Let God-Perfection
Guide your steps.
This is the only way
For you to proceed.

549. SMILE, HUMANITY, SMILE!

Smile, humanity, smile!
God not only loves you
Constantly
But also needs you
Unreservedly.
Smile, humanity, smile!

550. CONSOLATION

My body leaned to my soul in tears.
My soul consoled it and said,
"My little brother,
Is there anything
That I cannot do for you?
Is there anything
That I will not do for you?"

551. HEAVEN-LOVERS, EARTH-LOVERS

O Heaven-lovers,
Where are you?
Heaven has descended.
Why are you not greeting
Heaven-Beauty?

O earth-lovers,
Where are you?
Earth has ascended.
Why are you not greeting
Earth-purity?

552. LIFE'S NIGHT, LIFE'S DAY

Each life has a night;
Each life has a day.
The night of a life
Has silence in it.
The day of a life
Has sound in it.
Life's night, life's day
Complete and fulfil
God's stay on earth,
God's stay in Heaven.

553. I HAVE SURRENDERED TO THE TIMELESS

I have surrendered my heart
To the timeless in myself;
Therefore
I am happy.

I have surrendered my perfection-choice-life
To the timeless in myself;
Therefore
I am happy.

I have surrendered the seed of my past life,
The tree of my present life
And
The fruits of my future life
To the timeless in myself;
Therefore
I am happy.

554. THE WORLD WILL NEED YOU

Stand and wait;
The world will ignore you.
Walk and run;
The world will watch you.
Love and serve;
The world will admire you.
Pray and meditate;
The world will need you.

555. JUST MENTION HIS NAME

Just mention his name;
You will gain a free access
To God's entire Heaven-existence.

But try to be humble.
Otherwise, on your way to God's Palace in
   Heaven
You are bound to stumble.

556. WHEN I WORSHIP YOU

When
I worship You with folded hands
I get joy.

When
I love You with my heart's adoration-tears
I get greater joy.

When
I surrender to You
My desire-world
And
My aspiration-sun,
I get the greatest joy.

557. DO OWN ME

Do own me as Your own
To make me the prince of happiness.

Do own me as Your own
So that I can reach in You
My ultimate Source,
Delight.

558. DIE NOT, LIVE NOT

Die not!
God needs you on earth.
Live not!
Heaven's curious eye needs you in Heaven.

559. YOU CARE NOT

I clearly see that you care not
For earthly pleasures.
I clearly see that you care not
For heavenly joys.
I clearly see that you care not
For God-manifestation on earth.
You care only
For your own wisdom-manifestation on earth.

560. SWEET SILENCE-THOUGHT

Sweet silence-thought
I need you.
In you I see
Perfection-joy,
In you I feel
Divinity-breath,
With you I feel
God-manifestation-success.

561. LOVE AND PEACE

Peace proclaims:
Love is essential.

Love proclaims:
Peace is invaluable.

God proclaims:
Love within, peace without,
Are essential.

562. ALL GATES TO HEAVEN ARE OPEN

He is an honest mind.
He is a pure heart.
He is an illumining soul.
All gates to Heaven
Are wide open for him.
Sleepless he will sit
At the Feet of the Absolute Supreme.

563. YOU HAVE SEEN NOTHING

Have you seen the face of death?
Have you seen the throne of life?
Have you seen the farewell of the cosmic gods?
Have you seen love's armies?
No, you have seen nothing!
What you have seen is only
Failure's cry.

564. HE LOVES HIS DEATH

He loves his death.
He feels that death
Will give him some rest.
He feels that death
Will care more for him than life.
He feels that the other shore is greener.
He feels that a new experience
Will gladden him and fulfil him;
Therefore
His love for death
He treasures,
Expands,
Distributes.

565. WHAT IS MY FORCE?

What is my force?
My cry.

What is my force?
My surrender.

What is my force?
My oneness.

566. STAND A LITTLE FARTHER

Stand a little farther,
You intellectual fool!
Stand a little nearer,
You psychic God-child on earth!

567. TOO PROUD

Too proud to live with poverty on earth,
He wants to live in Heaven.

Too proud to die and make death the sovereign,
He does not want to go to Heaven.

568. THY LOVE IS MY NEST

O, Thy Love is my nest,
Thy Smile is my rest,
Thy Grace is my goal.

569. O FLOOD MY SLEEP

O flood my sleep
With Your Smile!

O love my life
With Your Beauty's Feet!

O bless my life
With Your Compassion-Vision!

570. KEEP ME INSIDE YOUR HEART

Keep me near Your Feet
If you want to make me
Happy.

Keep me inside Your Heart
If you want to make me
Happy,
Soulful
  and
Dutiful.

571. YOUR LIFE-GIVING SMILE

Father,
May I see Your life-giving Smile?

"Son,
I have shown it to you
Many, many times.
Once more I am showing it to you.
Love it and grow into
Its celestial fragrance."

572. MY HEART IS DROWNED IN YOUR JOY

My heart is drowned in Your Joy.
I cannot speak,
I cannot move.
Do give me only one thing more:
Your Compassion-Smile.

573. VAIN

Vain is my earth-struggle,
Vain is my Heaven-cry,
Vain is my sincerity-sigh,
Vain is my reality-search.

574. MY BEAUTY

My beauty is all there,
Inside my Lord.
I know it,
Yet I take the full credit
And the full glory.
Lord of Compassion,
Do grow sincerity inside my life.

575. WHEN WILL YOU COME AGAIN?

Lord, when will You come again?
"I shall come only when
Your heart becomes purity's moon,
Your mind becomes clarity's sky
And
Your life becomes duty's sun."

576. FIRST LOVE GOD

Father,
May I love Your humanity also?

"Certainly you can.
But first love Me,
Divinely,
Supremely,
Unreservedly
And unconditionally."

577. LORD, CLOSE MY MOUTH

Lord,
Close my mouth
Against ignorance-food.

Lord,
Open my mouth
To eat only
Perfection-preparation
And
Satisfaction-meal.

578. FATHER, YOU DECIDE

Father, please, You decide
Whether I shall go to Heaven
Or stay on earth.

"Stay on earth!
Here you have much to do
To please Me.
There you will go
Only to enjoy your well-earned rest-vacation."

579. MAKE MY LIFE

Make my life
From Your Perfection-Dream.

Make my soul
From Your Realisation-Reality.

580. ALL I WANT

A burning heart
Is all I want.

A loving smile
Is all I want.

A perfection-heart
Is all I want.

581. SOUL-WISDOM, MIND-WISDOM

Lord,
Draw me Heavenward
To Your Arms.
I need nothing more,
Nothing less.
My soul says
I am all Yours.
Only my mind says
Let us wait and see.

582. I NEED YOUR HEART

Lord,
Accept my sighs.
I need Your Heart
Of Compassion-Light
Badly.

"Son, I need your mind
Of confession-experience
So, so badly."

583. DO PLACE YOUR FEET IN MY HEART

Do place Your Feet
In my heart
So that I can feel the flood of Peace,
Kill the pride of ignorance-night
And see my oneness with
Your Dream-fulfilling Reality-form.

584. IF YOU JUST LOOK AT ME

My heart shall bloom
  into adoration
If You just once look at me.

My life-tree shall bear
Nectar-fruit
If You just touch it
With Your Benediction-Compassion-Feet.

585. ACCEPT MY LAST OFFERING

Accept my last offering
As You accepted
My first offering.

My first offering was
My ignorance-life.
My last offering is
My gratitude-heart.

586. HUMAN SENSES AND DIVINE SENSES

Human senses will satisfy
With success-beauty.
Divine senses will satisfy
With progress-necessity.

587. PATHWAYS

The path that leads to world-perfection
I saw.

The path that leads to God-Revelation
I saw.

The path that leads to God-Manifestation
I saw.

These roads are not so easy to walk along;
It takes time.
But devotedness to the Supreme will teach
   me how
To walk along these roads.

588. I EXPECT

I expect humanity to learn
From Heaven
The message of God-Justice
On earth.

I expect divinity to learn
From earth
The message of God-Compassion
And
The power of prevailing peace.

589. NEAR AND FAR

Humanly near
Is sincerity.
Divinely near
Is humility.

Humanly far
Is doubt.
Divinely far
Is indifference.

590. TO RAISE HUMANITY'S FAITH

Humanity has fallen.
How can he raise humanity's faith?
Only by showing humanity how to govern its
   life:
How to be the possessor of its prayer-life,
How to be the regulator of its meditation-life,
How to claim the Beloved Supreme as its very
   own.

591. BY A SINGLE ACT

By a single act of kindness
He can cure it
And make a new and good world.

By a single act of compassion
He can cure it
And make a better and truer world.

By a single act of self-sacrifice
He can create for himself and for others
The best of all worlds.

592. PROCLAIM THIS PERFECT MAN

Proclaim this perfect man
Whom humanity has knocked down.
He is rising,
He will rise,
He will forever rise.
He has become the governor of his own life.
His own power of prayer has made him
The best instrument of his eternal
Inner Pilot Supreme.

593. HE WHO SPEAKS FROM THE SUMMIT

I have not seen the path
That leads towards perfection.
Only he who speaks from the summit
Can embrace perfection-day.
In him the success-life
And the progress-soul
Together shall stay
To feed the face of ever-transcending
Satisfaction-sun.

594. JUSTICE AND COMPASSION

Justice is not the opposite of Compassion;
Compassion is not the opposite of justice.
Justice feels justified in perfecting imperfection.
Compassion feels justified in giving
A new chance,
A new hope,
A new dawn,
To the culprit in weakness-night.

595. HOW TO BE HAPPY

Unlimited activities
Cannot make you happy.
Devotedness to the Supreme
Only can make you happy.
If you learn from Heaven
Its all-seeing capacity,
You will be happy.
If you learn from earth
Its all-sacrificing capacity,
You will be happy.

596. BEYOND PEACE-EXPERIENCE

The curtains of her peace-room
Are drawn.
Her life is now beyond
Peace-experience.
She now tries to be wise
By becoming a learned fool.

597. YET HE LOVES ME

I failed to think,
I failed to thank,
I failed to love,
I failed to communicate,
I failed to breathe –
Yet God the Creator
Loves me,
God the Lover
Loves me,
God the Fulfiller
Loves me.

598. FAITH AND BELIEF

Faith can believe everything
That we say.
Belief can increase the strength
Of faith.
Belief is pure,
Faith is sure.
Belief looks around
To see the truth.
Faith looks within
Not only to feel the truth
But also to become the truth.

599. WHEN THE INNER BEAUTY SMILES

When the inner beauty smiles,
Love is bound to live.

When the inner duty smiles,
Oneness is bound to live.

When the inner concern smiles,
Perfection is bound to live.

600. I COULD NOT BELIEVE IT

His soul grew so fast
That I could not believe it.

His life grew so slowly
That I could not believe it.

His God became so close to him
That I could not believe it.

601. HIS MENTAL LIFE

His mental life is fast asleep.
It has to be aroused
And it must know
What its responsibilities are.

602. INDEED, IT IS A HAPPY DAY

Indeed, it is a happy day
Without any complaints.
Indeed, it is a happy day
Without a faint desire.
Indeed, it is a happy day
When the power of killing is replaced
By the power of loving.

603. WILL YOU FORGIVE?

Will you forgive what I have said?
Will you forget what I have said?
Will you remember what God said to you?
Will you remember what you always say to me?

604. GOD FORGAVE ME

God forgave me;
Therefore, I am with you.
I forgave the world;
Therefore, I am with you.
God has forgotten
My stupidity-night,
I have forgotten
My humiliation-night;
Therefore, I am with you.

605. GOD TOLD ME

God told me
In the year's morning
That this year
Progress and success
Together would try,
And they have.

606. UNANSWERED QUESTIONS

Heaven had a serious question.
Earth would not answer it.
What was the question?
"Is the soul less important
Or more important than the body?"
Earth remained silent.

Earth had a question
Heaven could not answer.
What was the question?
"Is God really partial to Heaven?"
Heaven remained silent.

607. INVITE YOUR SOUL

Invite your soul
To enter into your mind-jungle
To clear it up.

Invite your soul
To enter into your heart-insecurity
To strengthen it.

Invite your soul
To encourage you in all that you do and say.
Your soul will inspire you,
Fulfil you
And
Immortalise you.

608. BE AWARE!

Be aware of Heaven!
Heaven is mild, soothing, energising.

Beware of earth!
Earth is suffocating and dying.

609. ONE DAY'S REST

One day's rest
Gave him the strength of a giant.
One day's rest
Made him what he always wanted to be:
A man of Peace,
A man of all-fulfilling and all-nourishing
Peace.

610. LET US INVITE HIM

Here we have another guest:
Faithfulness.
Let us invite him.
His sweet presence
Brings us the hope of Paradise.
Let us invite him.

611. MESSAGE FROM MY SOUL

I sent my soul on a voyage.
It came back with this message:
Truth is not honoured,
Life is not valued,
God is not invoked.

612. O WILD ECSTASIES

O wild ecstasies of earth-life,
Live in the healing thoughts of beauty's life.
Measureless is your scope
To do the right,
To become the right
And
To awaken the light
In the sleeping, deathlessly sleeping, humanity.

613. SWEET SIMPLICITY

Sweet simplicity!
In you I see
The redeeming Grace of God.
In you I see
The silence-night of outer beauty.
In you I see
The calmness-quietude of inner beauty.

614. LIFE-ILLUMINING REALITY

Insecurity,
You are incomplete obscurity.
Impurity,
You are complete obscurity.
Purity,
You are life-illumining Reality.

615. TWO SPECIAL NEEDS

His fame and rumour together move.
He has a special need from Heaven
And also a special need from earth.
His special need from Heaven is
Compassion-Light.
His special need from earth is
Constant attention.

616. AIMLESS IS HE

After a lengthy reluctance
My doubt-friend at last wanted
To leave my abode.
Aimless is he in his absoluteness.

617. THE SOVEREIGNTY OF LOVE

The sovereignty of love nobody disputes.
The sovereignty of love is
   perfection-manifestation.
The sovereignty of love is the God-shrine
In his vision-temple,
In his earth-bound, sweet, immortal Height.

618. NO!

Must one become stupid
Before he becomes a man of knowledge?
No!

Must one become a beggar
Before he becomes the richest man on earth?
No!

Must one become a useless disciple
Before he becomes a first-class disciple?
No! no! no!

619. CULTIVATE TRUTH

This morning
My doubt failed to visit my Lord Supreme.
All reasons were insufficient,
Yet my Lord Supreme forgave my doubt
And said,
"Doubt, cultivate truth.
You will enjoy the harvest-beauty."

620. EVERYTHING IS MORTAL

Everything is mortal here.
Love is mortal,
Joy is mortal,
Concern is mortal,
Everything is mortal;
Therefore
Troubled is my Lord.
But a little surrender to God's Will
Makes everything immortal:
Love, Joy, Concern.
A little surrender to God's Will
Becomes Immortality itself.

621. IT'S YOUR TURN

It's your turn!
Look, all are watching.
Play the life-transformation-game well.
If you succeed,
Fastest will you run
Towards the Destination-Heights.

622. I FEEL MISERABLE

Here on earth
I cannot smile freely;
Therefore
I feel miserable.

There in Heaven
I cannot cry soulfully;
Therefore
I feel miserable.

Alas, neither Heaven nor earth
Comes to my rescue.

623. I SHALL DO IT FOR YOU

I shall do it for you.
I shall pray to God for you,
I shall meditate on you.
You need only allow me
To pray for you
And
To meditate on you.
Just do me that much favour.

624. THE WORST GUEST

Fear is a bad guest;
Nobody likes him.

Doubt is a worse guest;
Nobody likes him either.

Impurity is the worst guest;
Neither in Heaven
Nor on earth
Does anybody like him.

625. A NEW PHILOSOPHY

Now there is a new philosophy.
Where to look?
Look around,
Not within.
Where to start?
Anywhere you want to
Except from the very beginning!

626. DEATH

Whatever dies really does not die.
We see it not;
Therefore
We feel that it has died.
Death is only another shore
Of the Reality-sea.
Death is only another way
To God-Reality's Shore.

627. A WALL BETWEEN YOU AND GOD

My Lord has asked me to tell you
That He came to you
And got inside a small flower.
But He did not speak to you
Because he saw a wall between you
And Him.

628. I MUST NOT STAY HERE

Where the world is quiet
I must go.
Where all troubles have ended
I must go.
Here life is death;
I must not stay here.
There, death is death, life is life.
I must go, I must go.
There, life is life
And not, like here, sleep.
No, I must not stay here.

629. GOD APPARENTLY FORGOT HIM

Humanity betrayed him,
Divinity ignored him,
God apparently forgot him.
He therefore made friends
With ignorance-night.

630. HE DOES NOT HAVE THE FINAL WORD

Although he is superior to all,
He does not have the final word.
He asks his inner love of God
To play his role
And
He is always successful.

631. MAN'S FORGIVENESS

Man's forgiveness creates everything in you
Out of nothingness.
Man's forgiveness is a true believer in
   God-reality
In the heart of humanity, vast humanity.

632. GOD'S ECSTASY-LOVER

Before, he was a peace-lover.
Now he is a dynamo-lover.
A day will come when he will be purely
God's ecstasy-lover.

633. START AND STOP

Start loving!
You will swim.
Stop loving!
You will sink.
Start serving!
You will fly.
Stop serving!
You will drown in the core of ignorance-sea.

634. NOT KNOWING

Not knowing what to do
He made friends
With deep doubts.

Not knowing what to say
He invited the ugly-looking fear.

Now knowing whom to love
He loved his own self-form
Dearly and deeply.

635. THE HAPPINESS UNPARALLELED

Strengthen your heart's faith.
You will be happy.
Intensify your mind's God-hunger.
Yours will be the happiness unparalleled.

636. INSIDE THE HEART-GARDEN OF GOD

Because of my sincerity
They have lost me.
Because of my purity
I shall find them once again
Inside the Heart-Garden of God.

637. WE HAVE FOUND EACH OTHER

They have found me
Inside the Silence-Heart of God;
Therefore
They have become jealous.

I have found them
Inside the Sound-Life of God
Where
They have become treacherous.

638. SUCH IS HUMAN LIFE

Such is human life.
It only knows how to cry,
But
It accepts not consolation-light
From Heaven's smile-manifesting Reality.

639. ALL FOR YOU

Lord Supreme, all for You
My surrender-heart,
My concern-life,
My purity-body,
My devotion-soul.
All that I have is for You
To personally use.

640. THE FACE OF FALSEHOOD

The face of falsehood
I have seen many, many times.
Falsehood comes into existence
From the path of desire
And
From travels upon the path of desire.

641. YOU ARE A DREAMER

You are a dreamer,
But that doesn't mean you will become
A self-deceiving thought.

You are a dreamer,
But that doesn't mean you will become
A self-imposed authority.

You are a dreamer,
But that doesn't mean you will become
A God-fulfilling representative.

642. THE ETERNAL WATCHES

The Eternal watches time
And
Sees how long the seeker
Remains in the bosom of night.

643. DEATH'S FOOD

What is Death's food?
Death's food is
Ignorance-smile
And
Darkness-sigh
And
Unwillingness-surrender.

644. LUSTRE AND ECSTASY

God-Lustre grows, glows
And reaches the Height
Of the ever-transcending Beyond.

Ecstasy flows
And reaches the farthest corner
Of the Reality-globe.

645. GOD-LANGUAGE

Do you want to learn God-language?
God-language is
Aspire and give,
Give and aspire;
Delight achieve,
Delight distribute.
This is God-ecstasy immaculate;
This is God-language-delight.

646. O UNILLUMINED MIND

O mind of night,
O foul mind of life,
I have come to illumine you.

O night of the mind,
I have come to illumine you, too.

Let me illumine you both
In the Silence-Light of my transcendental
   Height.

647. GOD TOUCHES THE EARTH

God touches the earth
So everything will be possible.
Everything is being done;
Everything will be perfect,
Simply perfect,
For God touches the earth.

648. MY SOUL HAS TAUGHT ME

My soul has taught me
How to fly.
I have taught my soul
How to cry.

My soul has taught me
How to unlearn many painful things.
I have taught my soul
How to learn the world's excruciating pangs
And
How to remain in breathless pain.

649. LIFE AND DEATH ANNOUNCE EACH OTHER

Life announces death.
Life welcomes death,
For life is tired, exhausted
And wants to stop playing.

Death announces life.
But death is afraid of life.
Death sees Immortality-flow
In the stream of life.

650. GIVE TODAY ITS FULL VALUE

Don't throw your today
Against tomorrow.

Don't throw your today
Against yesterday.

Allow today to grow and glow,
To sing and dance in its own way.

Like yesterday, today too
Has much to contribute.
Like tomorrow, today too
Has much to contribute.
Give today its full value.
Let it play its role unhindered,
Unobstructed.
Let it play its role in full majesty,
Sovereign,
Alone.

651. THE EAR OF THE WORLD

The ear of the world
Is very big.
It hears everything.

The heart of the world
Is very small.
It does not contain anything.

The mouth of the world
Is big, big.
It devours everything,
Even though at times unnecessarily.

652. UNREAL SMILES

Earth's unreal smiles make me feel that
Earth is Deception-Queen.

Heaven's unreal smiles make me feel that
Heaven is Negligence-King.

My own unreal smiles make me feel that
The real smile can dawn
Only on the Face of our Beloved Supreme.

653. WHAT IS IT?

Joy, what is it?
It is its own security.

Security, what is it?
It is its own perfection.

Perfection, what is it?
It is the common satisfaction
Of humanity and divinity,
Of man and God.

654. WE SHALL ACCEPT AND TRANSCEND

As long as we live on earth
We shall have to accept certain limitations,
For earth is limitation itself.

Nevertheless, it is we who have to try
To transcend earth-limitations
As well as Heaven-Perfection.

655. O TEACHERS

O teacher of Hope,
I know your name.
Your name is Faith.

O teacher of Faith,
I know your name.
Your name is God's Grace.

O teacher of God's Grace,
You have a special name.
Your name is God's Silence-Reality
Manifested on earth
For humanity's salvation-light.

656. GIVE ME THE STRENGTH

Lord, give me the strength
To fall into Your Hands.
Give me the strength
To be pure in mind.
Give me the strength
To be secure in heart.

657. THE FINAL FREEDOM

He has gained the final freedom.
He must forsake idle thoughts
But
He will be happy for his blameless life.
He will be truly happy.

658. ENTIRELY DEPENDENT ON YOU

I am entirely dependent on You.
I shall become the air of Your immortal Bliss.
I shall become Your unconditional follower
   divine.
I shall maintain my unbroken hope.

659. MY LIFE-TRAIN

I saw my life-train weeping.
I cried with it.

I saw my life-train fainting.
I, too, fainted.

I saw my life-train eventually
Going in the right direction.
I smiled with it.

I saw my life-train reaching the destination.
I reached the destination with it.
And when I reached the destination
I saw that the destination was nothing other than
My aspiration-fulfilled crown.

660. AWAKE AND GATHER

Awake and gather,
Awake and gather,
Awake! The world needs you.
Gather! You need the world.
He who sees within
Discovers the reality
That God needs him.
He who sees without
Discovers the reality
That he needs God, God alone.

661. WHERE IS GOD'S SMILE?

Where do you find God's Smile?
Not in aspiration,
Not in realisation,
Not in perfection.
But
In the tears of gratitude-heart.

662. WHAT SHALL WE DO WITH THEM?

What shall we do with the little gods?
They tell us that they can cure us of our
Insecurity,
Impurity,
Jealousy.
Is it true?
We tell them,
"True, we have all these deplorable qualities,
But we wish to be cured not by you, O little gods,
But by the God Supreme, the Absolute Beloved
    Supreme.
Since you have free access to Him,
Please ask Him to cure our faults,
Our teeming imperfection-night."

663. TOO BIG, TOO SMALL

Lord, I am too small.
Perhaps, therefore,
You do not see me praying.

Lord, I am too big.
Perhaps, therefore,
You feel that I do not need
Your Presence white.

664. BLISSFUL IS MY LIFE

O Blessed Master,
Blissful is my life,
For my surrendered life
You have accepted as your own,
Very own.

665. TWO SPECIAL NAMES

He has two special names:
Fantastic rapidity
And
God's Compassion-Hand.

666. A MOMENT'S SWEETNESS

A moment's sweetness
Can change him and his life.

A moment's sweetness
Can verify earth's achievements.

A moment's sweetness
Can accelerate humanity's progress
Towards its destined goal.

667. A SPECIAL KIND OF SILENCE

He enjoys a special kind of silence.
This silence is called military silence.
This silence is dynamic;
This silence is progressive;
This silence expedites his reality's
   satisfaction-sky.

668. JOY

Joy in any earthly thing
Is very precarious.
Joy in any unearthly thing
Is not only soulful
But also fruitful.

669. O SILENCE

O silence,
Who says that you are an orphan?
No, never!
Your father is Eternity's self-transcending
   height.
Your mother is Eternity's self-penetrating
   depth.

670. YOU DO NOT LOVE THE REAL IN YOU

There was a time
When you were moneyless.
Now you are spiritless.
There shall come a time
When you will be worthless in everything.
Why?
Because you do not sing the glory
Of the real in yourself,
You do not love the real in yourself,
You do not care for the real in yourself.
The real in you
Is a God-life of ascending cry.

671. THEREFORE GOD LOVES YOU

You smile in dreams;
Therefore
God loves you.

You love in hatred;
Therefore
God loves you.

You do not sleep.
You manifest God
All the time
In every possible way;
Therefore
God loves you.

TRANSCENDENCE-PERFECTION

672. LORD, I THANK YOU

Lord, I thank You
For Your Smile.

I thank You
For my heart's cry.

I thank You
For all that You have done for me
And all that You have not done for me.

Lord, I thank You
Because You have given me
A sure heart,
A brave vital,
A pure mind
And a strong body.

Lord, finally, I love You
Because You have made me
Your Blessing-Love incarnate.

673. IN SILENCE SUPREME

In silence he came into the world.
In silence he went away.
In silence the world saw him
And loved him.
In silence Heaven needed him
And invoked him.
All done in Silence supreme.

674. YOU DO NOT KNOW, BUT GOD KNOWS

You do not know, but God knows
Whether I am good or bad.
You do not know, but God knows
Whether I love the world or not.
You do not know, but God knows
Whether I care for Heaven or not.
Only God knows.

675. AWAKE, YOU LAZY SLEEPERS

Awake, awake, you lazy sleepers!
Sing a song to the morning sun.
Appreciate, admire and adore
The inner flame,
The flame that is known as
The sweet land of liberty.

676. WITHIN AND WITHOUT

Dedication is within;
Celebration is without.
Cry is within;
Flight is without.
Surrender-light is within;
Conquering might is without.

677. HERE AND THERE

Here in the land of ingratitude
Alone I live.
There in the land of infinitude
Alone God lives.

Here I cry for God
In desert-heart.
There God cries for me
In Perfection-Palace.

678. DON'T LIVE IN A WORLD OF PROMISE

Don't live in a world of promise.
Live in a world of promise-fulfilment.
Don't live in the whisper of a dream.
Live in the manifestation of the dream-reality.

679. TAKE LIFE EASY

Take life easy,
For life is God's playground of transformation
And
Man's satisfaction-school.
Always take life easy.
This is the only way
To maintain
Serenity
In earth's mental asylum.

680. DO NOT BIND HIM

Do not bind him;
Let him go.
Let him go to Heaven
And live there
In infinite Peace,
Eternal Light
And
Immortal Bliss.
His Hour has come;
Let him go.
Do not bind him.

681. THEY KNOW NO REST

Your doubt-life knows no rest.
His fear-life knows no rest.
My hope-life knows no rest.
We three are always sailing
In the same boat.

682. I LIVE IN THE HOPE

I live in the hope of meeting Him.
I live in the hope of loving Him.
I live in the hope of pleasing Him.
I live in the hope of fulfilling
And manifesting Him.
I live, I live.

683. THEY HAVE FOUND THEIR WAY IN HIM

My heart has found its way in him;
Therefore
My heart is safe and happy.

My mind has found its way in him;
Therefore,
My mind is clear and confident.

My life has found its way in him;
Therefore
My life is soulful and fruitful.

684. WE LIVE IN EMPTINESS

Your beauty-eyes live
In an empty Eternity.
His power-arms live
In an empty Infinity.
My love-heart lives
In an empty Immortality.

685. LET US BE WISE

O earth,
Let us be wise.
You refrain from speaking ill
Of my Heaven-friend
And I shall refrain from speaking ill
Of your doubt-friend.

686. NO OTHER WAY

Improve your self-sufficiency
By virtue of God's
Compassion-Power.
There can be no other way,
Absolutely none.

687. OPPORTUNITY MISSED

Activity is self-perfecting opportunity.
Opportunity missed,
Ignorance-fee increased
Strikingly
And yet
Helplessly.

688. HEAVEN-HELPER, EARTH-LOVER

Yours is the soul
That helps Heaven.
Yours is the heart
That loves earth.

O helper of Heaven,
You are divinely great.
O lover of earth,
You are supremely good.

689. WHAT BELONGS TO GOD

What belongs to Heaven
My soul-light claims.
What belongs to earth
My heart-love claims.
What belongs to God
God asks my surrender-life to claim.

690. RE-EXAMINE YOURSELF!

Re-examine yourself!
If you pass this time,
Then your doubt-guest
And your fear-guest
Will immediately be compelled
To leave you;
Therefore I urge you
To re-examine yourself!

691. TWO THINGS HE NEVER FORGETS

He forgets often;
Therefore
He fails in everything he does
And says.
But two things
He never forgets:
His ceaseless love of God
And
His unparalleled oneness with God.

692. THE SONG OF DREAM-REALITY

I live in dancing dreams,
I live in weeping dreams,
I live in life-awakening dreams,
I live in earth-surrendering dreams,
I live in Heaven-descending dreams.
My life is the song of dream-reality
In the heart of earth,
In the soul of Heaven.

693. O ECHOES OF MY HEART

O echoes of my heart,
I love you.

O echoes of my heart,
I need you.

O echoes of my heart,
You make me feel
That I can challenge Eternity's Height,
Infinity's Light
And Immortality's Life.

694. HIS SPARKLING SMILE

His sparkling smile:
In that smile
The world grows and glows.
In that smile
A new world blossoms.
In that smile
Earth-suffering hears the message
Of fire-pure transformation,
Complete transformation.

695. THE SUN IS DANCING

The sun is dancing,
The moon is dancing,
The stars are dancing.
I am dancing this moment
With the sun, moon and stars.
Next moment I am sailing
With the sky.
The sky makes me feel
That I am the vastness of Infinity's Heart;
The sun, moon and stars make me feel
That God's creation is for ecstasy's
   beginningless birth
And endless journey.

696. THE RIVER OF MY HEART'S TEARS

The river of my heart's tears
Makes me feel
That this hour is nothing
But destruction-sigh.

The river of my soul's smile
Makes me feel
That indeed, this is the world of beauty,
This is the world of ecstasy.

697. I SHALL LIVE IN SATISFACTION-TRAIN

There was a time when I lived
In restlessness-train.

Now I live
In peace-train.

There shall come a time when I shall live
In satisfaction-train.

698. WHERE DO YOU LIVE?

Where do you live?
"I live in the paradise of tears."

Where do you live?
"I live in the tears of love."

Where do you live?
"I live in the friendship of divine tears."

699. SWEET MOMENTS

Sweet, sweet moments,
I wish to grow in you,
I wish to float in you,
I wish to fulfil myself with you,
With you.

700. ONLY ONE STORY IS NEW

Minds fight with minds;
That is not a new story.
Hearts love hearts;
That is not a new story.
Love is at times out of breath;
That is not a new story.
There is only one story which is new
And that story is:
Today's frustration-evening of man
Will be transformed
Into tomorrow's satisfaction-dawn of God.

701. EVERY TEAR

Every secret tear purifies
The human heart.

Every sacred tear illumines
The human life.

Every soulful tear immortalises
The human in us.

702. SWEETNESS AND DIGNITY

Sweetness tells me
I can love the world.
Dignity tells me
I can rule the world.
With sweetness we conquer the world.
With dignity we frighten the world.
Dignity surrenders to humility's sweetness
And finds there its satisfaction-abode.

703. THE BEAUTY OF TEARS AND SMILES

The beauty of tears
Changes human life sooner than at once.
The duty of smiles
Also changes human life sooner than at once.
The union of tears and smiles
Makes God and man embrace each other,
Fulfil each other
And satisfy each other.

704. THE DEPTH OF MY HEART

The flame of Light –
Where is it?
In the depth of my heart.

The beauty of Light –
Where is it?
In the depth of my heart.

The perfection of Light –
Where is it?
In the depth of my heart.

The satisfaction of Light –
Where is it?
In the depth of my heart.

The depth of my heart
Houses all the Light
In all its forms and shapes,
In all its beauties and delights.

705. MY YOUNGER SELF AND MY OLDER SELF

My younger self, ego,
Tells me that I can be happy
By being separated from the oneness-soul.
My larger self, oneness universal,
Tells me that there is no such thing
As ego-separativity.
It is all oneness-song,
Oneness-perfection,
Oneness-reality.
I and my older self together shall stay,
Together shall sing,
Together shall dance.

706. ONE CONSCIOUS SOUL

One conscious soul is more than enough
To arouse countless unconscious souls
From a comatose life of dark amnesia.

One conscious soul
Is God's representative
In God's unprecedented way.

707. THE SKY IS ALIVE

The sky is alive
With trumpets.
The sky is alive
With stars and planets.
The sky is alive
With the sun and the moon.
The sky is alive
With something else:
My satisfaction-light.

708. WHO CAN TOLERATE?

Who can tolerate
His sanctimonious devotion?
Who can tolerate
His false folded hands?
Who can tolerate
His intentional flickering of the eyes?
Who can tolerate
His insincerity-tongue?

709. DEAR HEART

Dear heart,
Come to the fore.
Your heart-life shall challenge
The flashes of thoughts.
You know well, perfectly well,
That yours is a soul
That has entire faith in the Lord,
The Absolute Supreme.

710. THIS IS YOUR NAME

Infinite Sweetness:
This is your name.
Infinite Beauty:
This is your name.
Infinite Reality:
This is your name.
Infinite Infinity, within and without:
This is your name.

711. MY HEART'S ETERNAL GUEST

Lord, I am with You always
And I love You always.
I drink Your Beauty always.
I smile at Your Eternity's Beauty always.
You are my heart's eternal Guest.
In You I see the centre of all excellence.
Lord Supreme, You are my heart-life
And my soul-light.
You are my Eternity's All.

712. HEART'S VISION IS WHAT MATTERS

The climbing heart's vision
Is what matters,
Not the mind's teeming confusion.
The heart embodies vision-light;
The mind indulges in confusion-desert-night.

713. LOVE SPREADS ITS WINGS

Real love, love divine,
Knows no delay.
Sooner than at once
It spreads its wings
All around the nest
Of God's created universe.

714. I HAVE FOUND YOUR NEST

O Lord,
In Your Eyes of Beauty
I have found Your Nest.
Delight is my name
When I live in Your Nest.
The heart of a singing bird
My life becomes
In song's world of silence.

715. DO ANYTHING YOU WANT

My soul I will pour
Into You:
Do anything You want to do with it.
Make me into either
The beauty of the morning
Or the ugliness of imperfection-night.
Do anything You want.

716. TUNE ME FOR LIFE

O Master-Musician,
Tune me for life again.
The awakening of new music
My heart wants to become.
My life is now mingled
In ecstasy's height.

717. IMMORTALITY BESTOWED

The starry Heavens
Come down to gaze upon me.
The voice of the morning birds
Bestows Immortality on me,
On my aspiration-heart.

718. GOD'S RAPTURE-FIRE

O mute despair,
I feel your suffering,
I feel your pangs.
Wait, have patience.
Your despair will be transformed
Into God's Rapture-fire.
Wait for God's choice Hour.

719. I DIE TO LIVE IN YOU

O Lord,
Only if You tell me
That You love me
Will I believe You.
I need only to die in You,
I die only to live in You.

720. THE KIND OF PERSON I AM

If you do not know the kind of person I am,
Then I wish to tell you.
I am a Truth-seeker,
A God-lover,
A God-revealer
And a God-fulfiller
On earth;
A God-dreamer
And a God-bestower
In Heaven.

721. REJECT ME NOT

O Lord Supreme,
Reject me not into the world again.
I have suffered, I am still suffering.
With each breath I breathe
Fires of wild destruction enter into me.
O Lord Supreme,
Reject me not into the world again.
I pray, I pray, I pray!

722. THIS VERY MOMENT

This very moment
Is the best the world can afford to give us.
Let us avail ourselves of this golden moment.
Inside the heart of the moment
Is Eternity's Silence-life
And Infinity's Smile.

723. LORD, I AM GRATEFUL

O Lord,
When You receive my prayer
I am grateful.
When You do not fulfil my prayer
I am grateful, too,
For I know that You know best what is good
    for me.
Dear Lord,
Only show me the path of real love,
The path of real light.

724. ILLUMINATION-FLOOD

To speak to the Lord Supreme
Is to commune with your own heart.
Who is your Lord Supreme, after all?
The illumination-flood
Of your own highest Self.

725. ECSTASY WITHIN, ECSTASY WITHOUT

This morning my Lord Supreme
Gave ears to my soulful words;
Therefore
Today my existence on earth
Has become ecstasy-flood,
Ecstasy within,
Ecstasy without.

726. HEAVEN SMILED TWICE

Heaven smiled at me twice:
Once when I criticised Heaven
For its careless indifference;
Once when I solemnly said
That I belonged to Heaven's silence
And not to earth's sound.

727. O MY ASPIRING HEART

Heart,
In you is my home;
In you is my all.
You are the preserver
Of all that is real in me.
You are my God-hunger,
You are my God-nourishment,
O my aspiring heart.

728. HIS SOUL IS ECLIPSED

His soul's light
Is eclipsed by his vital's desires.
He finds no more
His soul's beauty-height.

729. O SACRED SOUL-FLAMES

O sacred flames of my soul,
Do kindle my heart
And make it radiate with your light!

730. WHO KNOWS MAN'S FATE?

The soul in the soul
Immortal becomes.
The man in the man
Mortal becomes.
Who knows man's fate?
Who knows God's fate?
I know each man
Is tomorrow's blossoming God
And each God
Is tomorrow's manifesting man.

731. AN UNCERTAIN HOUR

An uncertain hour
Returned all his mental agonies,
All his teeming doubts
And
All his imperfection-nights.

An uncertain hour
Gave him back what he was
In the core of night.

732. A TIME WHEN I EXISTED NOT

There was a time when I existed not
As an individual ego.
I existed only as universal Reality-light
And transcendental Vision-light.

733. A GLORIOUS VICTORY

Fear and doubt
Come and go.
You know them one and all.
They do not fascinate us;
They attack us and weaken us.
They tell us what to do
And where to go.
They try to make us their own.
If they succeed, we lose
In the battlefield of life.
If they lose, we win
A glorious victory.

734. THIS TIME I AM GOING TO WIN!

This time I am going to win!
I shall not lose to ignorance-night.
This time I am going to win!
All misunderstandings between reality and me
I have cast aside.
Without fail I am going to win
In the battlefield of life!

735. LET ME PUT IT THIS WAY

Let me put it this way:
My aspiration is followed
By progress-light.
My desire is followed
By success-night.

736. ALL I HAVE TO DO

All I have to do is to accept it
Without understanding.

All I have to do is to believe it
Without knowing.

All I have to do is to surrender to it
Without discovering.

737. I WILL DO IT FOR FREE

Earth, I will do it for free.
I will help you increase
Your aspiration-cry for Heaven abundantly.
I will do it for free.

Heaven, I will do it for free.
I will help you increase
Your compassion-light for earth generously.
I will do it for free.

738. HIS VERY PRESENCE

His very presence
Creates a great burst of surprise
On earth.
He died to make all
See their past.
His heart makes all
Feel their oneness with the Vast.

739. YOUR SOUL'S WISHES

You will refuse to own yourself,
You are such a coward!
This is not something that your soul wants.
Your soul wants you to accept your life,
Discipline your life,
Fulfil your life.
Your soul wants nothing but that.

740. THE EASIEST THING

To call you my Master
Is the easiest thing,
And I have done it already.
To call you my all
Is also the easiest thing,
And I have done it already.
But to call you my human friend
Is the most difficult thing,
And I will never succeed in doing it,
Never!

741. SMILE, AMERICA!

Smile, America, my America,
Smile!
Why do you weep, why do you cry?
The world's volley of criticism
Need not curse the real in you
And
It cannot curse the real in you.
Smile, America!
Run and jump!
Fly!
Achieve and become!
Smile, America, smile!

742. FREEDOM AND FRIENDSHIP

Freedom we want,
Friendship we want.
Freedom from bondage,
Friendship with all and sundry.
Freedom and friendship
Together complete the game.

743. PREPARATION FOR PEACE

Preparation for peace is needed,
But where?
At home?
No.
In the inmost recesses of one's heart?
Yes.
Peace-seed must be sown in the heart.
Then only it will grow
In the body of human life.

744. AN UNNOTICED BONDAGE-CHAIN

If liberty springs up spontaneously,
It is liberty.
If not,
It is an unnoticed bondage-chain,
An unrecognised bondage-frustration.

745. YOU CANNOT CHEAT THE PURE

You can cheat the brave
If you want to,
But you cannot cheat the pure,
For in the heart of the pure
God's all-illumining Vision looms large.

746. QUALITY OR QUANTITY?

America: quality or quantity?
Both quality and quantity!
America's heart of light is quality.
America's mind of wisdom is quantity.

747. I HAVE GIVEN YOU MY LIFE

Lord Supreme, I have given You my life.
Let my heart always remain young
So that it can run towards You.
I know Your Protection will always save me
And my all.

748. I KNOW THERE IS FORGIVENESS

O Lord Supreme,
If it is too difficult for You to love me,
No harm.
Just allow me to love You.
I do not want to be loved
If it is not Your Will.
I truly know
I have done my best.
I have tried to please You
According to my capacities
And
According to my limitations.
But I always say, I always know,
That there is forgiveness,
Constant forgiveness.

749. I CANNOT WALK ALONE

Lord Supreme,
Grant me aspiration-cry.
Cover my weakness
If so is Your Will.
If not, expose me to the world at large.
I cannot walk alone.
I need Your Protection-Light.
Give me the courage to trust the life
Of each unknown hour.

750. LIVE IN THE DAY OF BLOOM

Live not in the heavy day of doom.
Who asks you to live in the heavy day of doom?
Live in the light day of bloom,
Live in the joy of beauty's smile,
Live in the joy of Immortality's glorious dawn.

751. EVERYTHING WILL BE ALL RIGHT

Wait with patience.
Everything will be all right.
Wait with hope.
Everything will be all right.
Wait with conviction.
Everything will be all right.

752. AN OBLIGATION-FREE LIFE

Do you want to live an obligation-free life?
Then come to me.
I shall show you where you can find
An obligation-free life.
An obligation-free life is found
Only in the heart of oneness-perfection,
In God-acceptance of man
And man-acceptance of God.

753. WHO HAS DONE IT?

The tree of life is beautiful.
But who has made it beautiful?
It is the faith of the seeker.
Who has given the faith to the seeker?
God, the unconditional Lover Supreme.

754. TEACH ME TO BUILD

O Lord Supreme,
Teach me to build and not to break.
Then I shall learn to behold
Thee and Thy Duty.
Then shall my soul learn to stand in
    Thy Presence
With adoration-flame.

755. MY HEART-DOOR

I cannot close my heart-door,
For I know not when my Beloved Supreme
   will arrive.
I cannot leave my heart-door open,
For who knows who will come in?
My heart-door must remain open
Only for my Beloved Supreme.

756. NEW HOPES

New hopes of Heaven have touched
Earth-arena.
We have no reason to deny ourselves.
Pure we feel in each other's hearts.

757. GOD-PROMISE

God-promise never fails;
Yet
In bitter separation
We listen to God-Promise.

758. JUST TO LIVE IN THE HEART

O Supreme,
Just to live in the heart I cry.
Just to live in the heart I die.
With a child's heart I cry.
To whom do I turn?
To Thee, to Thee, to Thee alone.
Only to live in Thee, I die.

759. NOW IT ALL DEPENDS ON YOU

Now it all depends on You.
Don't trick me any more.
I shall joyfully,
Eternally cling to You,
To You alone.

760. I SHALL NEVER BE DISTRESSED

I have already instilled peace in my heart;
Therefore
I shall never be distressed.
To You I have already offered
The flower of my heart's expression.

761. CREATE ME ANEW

Create me anew once more.
Until You call on me,
Dissatisfied I shall always remain.
Teach me,
Teach my heart to cling only to You.

762. ALL SHALL BE MENDED

All that is broken shall be mended
Without fail.
That is true beyond this momentary suffering
Of doubt-separation from God.

763. I SPORTED WITH YOU

Down the path of hope
I sported with you today.
I shall not deprive the divine child within me
Of anything, any day.

764. I SHALL PROCLAIM AND PERFORM

I shall proclaim the love,
I shall perform the task.
In me Your matchless Beauty shall sparkle,
Full of honey Sweetness-Light.

765. AMERICA HAS BECOME GREAT

Two centuries have rolled by.
America has become greater than the greatest.
How?
By always keeping the eternal God-child in her
To the fore.

766. THE HOUR HAS STRUCK

The hour has struck.
Nobody can doubt that this world is God's.
This world belongs to
God the Doer,
God the Action,
And God the Witness.

767. WHEN THE HOUR COMES

When the hour comes,
Who can doubt?

When the hour comes,
Who can remain aloof?

When the hour comes,
Who can deny?

When the hour comes,
Who can remain untransformed?

When the hour comes,
Who can remain without becoming
 perfection-glow?

768. LET NOTHING STOP THEM

My soul will go to You
Without fail.
Let nothing stop it!

Your Soul will come to me
Without fail.
Let nothing stop it!

769. WHAT MORE CAN YOU DO?

O American soul,
What more can you do?
You are already ready.
You know the way.
You are already running.
The goal is nearing.

770. THE BEST OF EVERYTHING

America has the best of everything
Because its heart has housed the many
And allowed them to live freely
In their own way.

771. WITHIN ME DESCEND

Heavenly Father,
Within me descend.
In me is the love
That illumines the universe.
In me is the joy
That cheers the human heart.

772. O FOUNTAIN OF FLAME

God, open the door
Of my mental peace.
O Fountain of Flame divine,
I shall become a true Yogi.

773. I SHALL WAIT FOR YOU

I was at the Feet of Silence.
I was going to offer my body,
My mind,
And my ability.
But I shall wait a day
For you.

774. AWAKEN MY HEART

Awaken my heart,
O Lord Supreme,
My Father Eternal.

Enter into my soul,
O all-illumining,
All-loving heart.

775. AWAKE, O EARTH

O unawakened earth, awake!
Challenge the skies' commotion.
Conquer ignorance and pain.
Fulfil yourself in the march of time.

776. PAINFUL IT IS TO SEE

Painful it is to see
The empty heart's fear.

Painful it is to see
The insecure heart's pangs.

Painful it is to see
The weak heart's friendship with the base vital.

Painful it is to see
The unaspiring heart's slow movement
Towards the Golden Shore.

777. O SACRED PURITY

O sacred Purity,
You tell me that I can eventually become
God's Life-Breath.

O sacred Purity,
You tell me that I can eventually become
Man's salvation-giver.

778. ASPIRE!

Aspire!
If not, everything will follow
The ancient dust.

Aspire!
If not, earth will not claim you;
Heaven will disown you.

Aspire!
God the Reality in you
Desperately needs you.
God is longing
For His complete, perfect Manifestation
In the heart of earth's imperfection-ignorance.

779. I AM BUT A PETAL

I am but a petal
Of the morning rose.
I see the morning sky.
For me the morning sun glows,
In me God's Hope-Light grows,
With me Infinity's Beauty-Smile flows.

780. O TEMPTATION-SERPENT

O temptation-serpent,
Do you think you will be able to conquer me?
O temptation-serpent,
Do you think that I will surrender to you?
O temptation-serpent,
"Your transformation-day is nigh,"
Declares humanity's perfection-smile
In the heart of temptation-destruction-volcano.

781. O BEAUTY, O PURITY

O Beauty,
Your purity is your divinity.

O Purity,
Your beauty is your perfection.

O Beauty, O Purity,
You two are my friends eternal.
Beauty, with you I go to Heaven.
Purity, with you I live on earth.

782. BEAUTY

Beauty's pulse
The seeker feels.

Beauty's face
The seeker sees.

Beauty's glory
The seeker grows into.

Beauty's perfection
The seeker ultimately becomes.

783. THE FAITHFUL AND THE FAITHLESS

He forgave the faithless ones;
Therefore
He is happy.

He loved the faithful ones;
Therefore
He is happy.

He became one with
The suffering of the faithless ones
And
The joy of the faithful ones;
Therefore
He is triumphantly happy.

784. MY SOUL LONGS FOR YOU

Sweet Beloved, come to me.
My soul longs for You,
Always for You,
To render You singlehearted
Devoted service.

785. YOUR ETERNITY'S HOME

O Lord Supreme,
You have made me live
In the garden of happiness-light.
Now one more boon do grant me:
Do make my heart
Your Eternity's beloved Home.

786. FILL MY TEMPLE OF LIGHT

Heavenly Father,
Awaken my heart,
Ignite my age-long darkness,
Fill my Temple of Light
With Your Fragrance-Beauty.

787. TEACH ME TO WORSHIP WITHIN

Teach me to worship within.
I shall try to obey my inner voice.
I shall also strive to know Thee
In the outer life of manifestation-joy.

788. I AM A LION

O Lord Supreme,
Please tell me that I am a lion,
Not a sheep.
I must roar with
All-conquering courage.
O Lord Supreme,
If You tell me
I will believe You.

789. YOU ARE SO NEAR

You are so near to me.
I shall fulfil You.
I shall and I can.
I can and I shall.

790. NO EVIL CAN BEFALL ME

No evil can befall me.
Nothing can hurt my soul.
His Heart of Love shelters me.
Ah, God is so near
To humanity's sky
And Divinity's Smile!

791. WHAT I HAVE LEFT

Lord Supreme,
In the morning You counted my tears.
In the evening You heard my songs.
Now at night I give You what I have left:
A pure,
Serene
And spontaneous love.

792. ONLY FOR YOUR SIGHT

Lord, You have accepted me
Out of Your Compassion-Height.
I hunger and thirst
Only for Your sight
At every moment
Of my wakeful hours.

793. WHAT CONCERNS ME

Failure does not concern me.
What concerns me is God-satisfaction
In God's own Way
In my aspiration-life.

794. THE WORLD SUFFERS

To have no belief is to suffer.
The world suffers from lack of belief
In the Pilot within.

To have wrong belief is to suffer.
The world suffers from wrong belief
About the Pilot within.

795. DO NOT DISTURB

Do not disturb
The sleep of death.
Do not disturb
The duty of life.
Do not disturb
The necessity of God-Compassion-Light.

796. HEAVEN-BREATH

When you breathe from Heaven
You feed the hungry heart
And the thirsty soul
Of earth.

797. THE ARMS OF FATE

All around me I see the arms of fate.
Within me is idleness supreme.
I am reluctant
To do my Master's will.

798. AN ANCHOR SURE AND SAFE

I have an anchor
Sure and safe.
Perils can never lurk within my deeps.
I am all secured
By my Saviour's adamantine Will.
In me once again
Love's purest joy
Is permanently restored.

799. THE SEEKER-SOUL

The seeker-soul
Was in love
With supreme Joy;
Therefore
Death did not dare to interfere,
And
Immortality grew
Inside the seeker
And his heart of joy.

800. CHANCES AND CHOICES

Life is composed of
Chances and choices.
He who surrenders to God's Will
Receives the blessing of choices.
And he who does not
Surrender to God's Will
Surrenders to the chances of fate.

801. THE RICHES OF GOD'S GRACE

His earth-life is feasting
On the riches of God's Grace.
His prayer to God:
"Lord Supreme, keep me singing
Your Victory-Song
As I proceed along the road of Eternity.
My Lord Supreme,
No more do I see life's dreary waste.
No more do I see life's countless thorns.
I see only my strength,
My beauty,
My soul's joy
And my Eternity's All."

802. YOU HAVE FORGIVEN ME

Lord Supreme, You have forgiven me.
You have forgiven the teeming lapses
Of Your servant.
I am always intoxicated by beauty's love.
But You have made me immaculate.
My gratitude-heart I have offered to You
And You have offered me Your Promise-Light.
You have accepted the animal in me,
The human in me,
The divine in me
As Your very own.

803. HIS WORLD

His world is now
In the Smile of God.

His world is now
In the cry of man.

His world is now
In the satisfaction
Of his Godward march.

804. O VOYAGER OF TIME

O voyager of time,
Onward you proceed
And offer to the world
Your achievement-light.
Much have you to discover;
Much have you to offer,
O voyager of time.

805. WHAT AM I?

What am I?
A tear shed by an angel.

What shall I be?
The Light that climbs
To the highest Height.

806. THE ART OF BELIEVING

O Lord Supreme,
I have learned the art of believing.
Will You not teach the art of believing
To my old friend, my ex-friend,
Disbelief?

807. ONE WHO TRULY LOVES GOD

One who truly loves God
Need not ask God for any favour,
For God knows what is best for him.
God gives him His exalting Sweetness,
His illumining Kindness,
His fulfilling Oneness-Light.

808. WHO WILL SAVE WHOM?

Who will save whom?
The self-destroying man
Caught in his own destruction dance –
How is he going to save the world?

809. O DUST

O dust, I salute you,
I love you,
For you have never deceived me,
And will never deceive me.

810. O BEAUTY'S PEACE

Sleep, sleep, O Beauty's peace,
Sleep within me.
I shall give you a song from Eternity's
   Songbook.
Sleep, sleep within me.

811. IMAGINATION AND REASON

Imagination does not
Care for reason.

Reason does not
Care for imagination.

The poet in me cries
For imagination-wings.

The philosopher in me cries
For reason-sword.

812. MIND-TRAVELLER, HEART-TRAVELLER

O my mind-traveller,
You cannot go very far.
Your vision is very narrow.

O my heart-traveller,
The length and breadth of the world
Is too narrow for you,
For you far transcend
The length and breadth of the world.

813. DOUBT

Doubt, you have no right
To experiment with life.
Doubt, you have no right
To experience life.

Doubt, you have the right
Only to experience life's disobedience and
   confusion —
Its self-contradiction-night.

814. BORN IN THE LAND OF DREAMS

He was born
In the land of dreams.
But now he lives
In the core of reality,
For he is caught by the golden net
Of humanity's cry.

815. MERRILY, MERRILY

Merrily, merrily
I shall spend my life.

Merrily, merrily
I shall enjoy myself in sleep.

Merrily, merrily
Immortal day within me shall grow.

Merrily, merrily
The ancient trees within my heart shall climb.

816. THE JOYS OF NIGHT AND DAY

From the joy of night
I sing the song of innocence.
From the joy of day
I sing the song of capacity.

817. PARADISE

Concern is the high
Paradise.
Love is the higher
Paradise.

Oneness is the highest
Paradise.
Doubt is the lowest
Paradise.

818. BETWEEN PUNISHMENT AND FORGIVENESS

Between punishment and forgiveness
What do I want?
I want both, if necessity demands.
If by punishing me, O Lord,
You can expedite my life's journey
Towards Your Golden Shore,
Then punish me by all means.
I want not Your Compassion-Forgiveness-Light.

819. THE MARRIAGE OF HEAVEN AND HELL

Where is the marriage
Of Heaven and Hell?

The marriage of Heaven and Hell
Is in the mind's dry desert
And in the heart's loving nest.

820. BEHIND ALL SHADOWS OF ADVERSITY

Behind all shadows of adversity
There is prosperity.
Wait and see!

Beauty's Infinity,
Infinity's Beauty
Will clasp you behind all shadows
Of adversity-night.

821. THE BECKONING OF SILENCE-LIGHT

I know not the depth of my fulness.
But I see the beckoning of silence-light,
Where fulness abides,
Where plenitude and infinitude abide.

822. GRACE AND SERVICE

Love is the grace
Which you can add
To your service-life.

Grace added to service
Makes perfection blossom
In the twinkling of an eye.

823. CAPACITIES

The capacities of an undying mind
I had.
The capacities of a loving heart
I have.
The capacities of a surrendered life
I shall have.

824. SWEET WAS LIFE

Sweet was life,
And sweeter as the years went by.
Full and perfect ease belonged to him
When he saw all around him
The arms of faith.

825. DEATH AND LIFE

Death was watching him;
Therefore
He was hiding.

Life is watching him;
Therefore
He is singing and dancing.

826. WHY DO YOU NEED ME?

Why do You need me, Lord?
"Son, I need you because
With you I shall face
My ever-transcending Beyond,
For you I shall play
My cosmic Game,
In you I shall see
My Dream-Reality and My Reality-Dream."

827. THEIR SORROWS

The artist's sorrow:
Nobody appreciates his painting.

The poet's sorrow:
Nobody reads his book.

The philosopher's sorrow:
Nobody accepts his philosophy.

The seeker's sorrow:
Nobody takes him seriously.

828. INSIDE OUR HEARTS

I shall not die, but live.
Where?
Inside your heart.

I shall not speak, but listen.
Where?
Inside my heart.

829. MORE THAN ENOUGH TIME

Do not count the time you have lost,
But count the time
That is at your immediate disposal.
The time that is before you
Is more than enough
To enter into Infinity's Heart
And Eternity's Perfection-Delight.

830. I SIMPLY DO IT

I simply do
What many dream of.
I simply do
What others talk about.
I simply become
What others dare not even to imagine.

831. HE FACED LIFE AND DEATH

He faced death with success.
He faced life with progress.
He waited for the proper end of death
In Immortality's flow
And
Infinity's silence-glow.

832. DON'T INSULT GOD ANY MORE

Don't dare insult God any more.
Enough! Enough!
Although He is far beyond the reach
Of human insult,
Humanity must not increase its
 ignorance-night
By deliberately speaking ill of God,
The eternal Dreamer,
The eternal Beloved,
The eternal Lover Supreme.

833. I MISUSED INFINITY

There was a time when Eternity was mine.
Alas, now I have only the ephemeral.

There was a time when Infinity was mine.
Alas, now I am forced to be satisfied with the finite.

I misused Eternity;
Therefore Eternity has left me.

I misused Infinity;
Therefore Infinity has left me.

Now I am misusing the finite;
Therefore the finite moment also will leave me soon.

834. CONCERN AND CARE NEEDED

Each thing on earth
Needs and deserves
Concern and care.
Concern and care not offered,
Love immediately forfeited.

835. LOVE FIRST

Think first,
See afterwards.

Love first,
Fight afterwards.

Become the truth first,
Speak afterwards.

836. FOOD FOR THE SOUL

The body's food
Is matter-made.
The soul's food
Is spirit-made.
Gratitude-life,
Gratitude-heart for God
Is food for the soul.
Perfection-cry
Is food for the soul.
Heart's awakening
Is food for the soul.

837. FROM AGE TO AGE

From each age to each age, O Lord,
You come into the world.
Yet we enjoy living in oblivion-cave.

Still, O Lord, You come
To wipe our tearful eyes
And make us feel that You love us
And
You need us.

838. WHERE THERE IS DOUBT

Where there is doubt
There is no smile of love.
Where there is doubt
There is only self-contradiction
And
Self-annihilation.

839. YOU HAVE ALL

O mind,
You have all the crowning thoughts.
O heart,
You have all the soulful thoughts.
O life,
You have everything:
Suffering-world,
Struggling-world,
Striving-world,
Imperfection-world,
Ingratitude-world.

840. REVEAL AGAIN THE LIGHT

Lord Supreme, reveal again the light.
This time I shall treasure the light
And grow into the illumining fragrance
Of Your Light infinite.

841. CONVICTION ACCELERATES

Patience knows not the hour.
Hope imagines the hour.
Conviction not only knows the hour
But accelerates the arrival of the hour.

842. THIS WORLD BELONGS TO THE CREATOR

The Hour has struck.
All human doubts have vanished.
All human hesitations are illumined.
This world of ours belongs to the Creator,
The Beloved Supreme.

843. THE HEART OF MY GRATITUDE-SEA

Lord Supreme, Absolute Supreme,
Father Supreme, Beloved Supreme,
With Your infinite Bounty I started
To compete with my previous achievements.

I have far surpassed my previous achievements.
Now the golden fruit
I place at Your Feet.

In me, through me, You have achieved
This humanly unbelievable achievement.
But divinely, it was not only possible but
   inevitable.

This is not a miracle, O Lord,
This is just a reality-experience
Which inspires me to transcend
What I have
And what I eternally am.

O Beloved Supreme,
In absolute Silence-Light
To You I offer
The heart of my gratitude-sea,
The breath of my oneness-sky.

APPENDIX

EDITOR'S PREFACE TO THE FIRST EDITION

Using concentrative powers developed through meditation, Sri Chinmoy wrote the 843 poems in this volume in a 24-hour period – from midnight to midnight on 1 November 1975. This surpasses his previous record of 360 poems written in one day on 28 April of last year and published under the title *The Goal Is Won*.

When Sri Chinmoy endeavours to set new records of this kind, he does so out of childlike enthusiasm, for the pure joy of it. Also, such achievements become a means for inspiring humanity and demonstrating how much a human being is capable of when he invokes God to work in and through him.

Several of Sri Chinmoy's disciples remained with the Master throughout the writing marathon, transcribing the poems from his handwritten notebooks or from his dictaphone. Others worked around the clock at the printing press, and the book in its final printed form was completed less than 24 hours after the volume was finished.

FIRST EDITION PRINTING

This edition is a faithful reproduction of the first edition of Transcendence-Perfection, 1975.

[Note: Two printings of *Transcendence-Perfection* are extant, both published by Agni Press in 1975. The earlier printing is slightly different, as set out below.]

28. THREE METHODS

The human method
Begins by doubting.

The divine method
Begins by loving.

The supreme method
Begins by discovering,
    by serving.

37. BEAUTY, LUSTRE, ONENESS

Beauty
Is earth-satisfaction.

Lustre
Is Heaven-perfection.

God-satisfaction
Is earth-transformation:
God in all, for all.

216. I AM DYING

Lord, save me,
I am dying.

"Son, smile!
I am crying."

301. ALL I HAVE TO MY NAME

All I have to my name
Is Your Compassion-flood.
All I have to my name
Is Your Concern-sky.

BIBLIOGRAPHY

Sri Chinmoy:
— *Transcendence-Perfection*, Agni Press, NY, 1975.

TABLE OF CONTENTS

Transcendence-Perfection
Transcendence-Perfection   1

Appendix
Editor's preface to the first edition   411
Note on first edition printings   413
Bibliography   415

Table of contents   417

www.ingramcontent.com/pod-product-compliance
Lightning Source LLC
Chambersburg PA
CBHW030108240426
43661CB00031B/1330/J